/thē·il·logical/

S. James   D. Harold

Copyright © 2013 by S. James and D. Harold

All rights reserved. No portion of this book may be reproduced, stored in a retrieval system, or transmitted in any form or by any means—electronic, mechanical, photo-copy, recording, scanning, or other—except for brief quotations in critical reviews or articles, without the prior written permission of the publisher.

ISBN-13: **978-0615783208**
ISBN-10: **0615783201**

Visit us at www.the-illogical.com

All scriptures are quoted using the *New International Version* unless otherwise specified.

Blue House / Magoo

Denver · St. Petersburg · Dubai

The stage is set...

For centuries humanity has faced a myriad of religious choices. And Jesus has been one among many.

But what exactly did Paul mean when he said, "It is for freedom that Christ has set us free?"

What if the choice for humanity has always been between *freedom* and *everything else*?

Jesus said, "Come to me, *ALL* who are weary and burdened, and I will give you rest."

ALL who are tired of religion (any religion); weary of appeasing gods and spirits while 'trying' to be good.

ALL who are tired of being shackled under the tyranny of finite human resources and the limited resources of the physical world.

ALL who are tired of guilt-trips and striving in 'sanctification' toward 'Christlikeness,' and *ALL* big-time sinners who don't really care what anyone thinks.

ALL who are tired of *ALL THAT CRAP*...and want to *rest*.

For 2,000 years, God has been inviting the world to *freedom*.

God invites you to join his party.

And the party starts now.

Table Of Contents
-Episode One-

Scene 1	Another Brick in the Wall	1
Scene 2	Our Flat Earth Has Always Been Round	8
Scene 3	Ordinary People	16
Scene 4	So This Blind Man With No Arms and No Legs Walks Into a Bar...	27
Scene 5	...And Says, "Excuse Me, Gotta Drink For a Man On His Way To Heaven?"	37
Scene 6	Walking the Spiritual Plank	46
Scene 7	The Narrow Road *Never* Traveled	57
Scene 8	"The Wise Man" Keeps in Context	66
Scene 9	"Respect My Authori-TIE!"	73
Scene 10	Burdened Under the Lightness of Being	85
Scene 11	Every Time I Sea Food, I Eat It!	93
Scene 12	Excommunicated From My Church For Not Upholding the Law of Moses	103
Scene 13	Christians in God's Torture Chamber?	113
Scene 14	No Country For Old Thinking	122

-Episode Two-

Scene 15	Give Me That Ole' Testament Justice	133

Scene 16	Are We All a Bunch of Crazy Galatians?	145
Scene 17	I Misinterpret When I Don't Try To	159
Scene 18	The Big Miss	171
Scene 19	Why Can't "Big Brother" Just Leave Me Alone?	188
Scene 20	Laws to Protect Your Ass (well, your donkey, that is)	193
Scene 21	I Will Choose….Free Will	200
Scene 22	I Took a Guilt-Trip and Forgot To Pack My Underwear	207

-Episode Three-

Scene 23	James and the Giant Misinterpretation	214
Scene 24	Show Me Yours, I'll Show You Mine	222
Scene 25	Sit the *F Down, and Shut the *F Up	239
Scene 26	God: "I Got Yer Back"	245
Scene 27	I Came Out of Gallbladder Surgery Missing My Left Leg	252
Scene 28	Without My Left Leg, I Now Walk With a Limp	260
Scene 29	Bless Me Father, For I Have Misinterpreted Confession	265

Conclusion:	Power, Authority, and Freedom	276
Appendix 1		286
Appendix 2		292

Forward by Brian Allen

The man who invented fire had a great tool for light and warmth.

He used it all the time and probably made a lot of friends. Soon it became known to everyone how to make fire for light and warmth.

Fire had changed the world.

But let's consider the more obscure day when the man's pet chicken wandered a little too close to the fire pit and fell to its fiery death.

How sad the man must've been—until he smelled roasted chicken for the first time!

He must've thought, "I've lost my pet chicken to the flames, but it smells so good! Could it taste that good?"

And...Yes, it did! The first hot meal was served (with coleslaw and mashed potatoes).

My point is this- Fire had always been useful for light and warmth. But now it served a greater purpose—for cooking food.

The discussion that will come from this book should not be about a reinvention of light or warmth, but about something that has been there all along, just waiting to be discovered.

I know the authors of this book personally, and to replace one dogmatic view of theology with another is far from their goal. In fact, 10, 50, 100 years from now, God may make things even more clear than what's presented in this book.

And yes, I realize the first human to cook over fire probably did not speak English.

Important Terms Used in This Book

Religion – Living apart from God in our own strength, power, and energy to follow rules and rituals, with the goal to appease God, and/or reconcile ourselves to God, and/or 'grow' toward God.

DOI – The descendants of Abraham through his son Isaac. The term DOI will be used for most of the book instead of 'Jewish' as the authors feel 'Jewish' has been so loaded down over the centuries with religious, political, economic, sociological, psychological and historical baggage as to mean things possibly not intended. The term DOI will be used throughout the book in the strictest ethnic and ancestral sense.

/thē·*il*·logical/ – Undoing centuries of cramming theological square pegs into round holes.

-Episode One-

Shackled!

The Two-Fold Mission of Jesus

Question

Have you ever read certain passages in the Bible and thought, *something doesn't seem quite right*, but you couldn't put your finger on it?

I have.

Sometimes I've listened to people teaching the words of Jesus and thought, *that doesn't quite line up with Paul later in the New Testament.*

For upwards of 40 years my faith has been able to withstand the clunks and bumps of scripture, however, something in the back of my mind has always itched, always whispered that something seems out of whack.

For instance, let's compare Romans 8:1 with Matthew 18:34-35:

> Romans 8:1—"Therefore, there is now no condemnation for those who are in Christ Jesus."

> Matthew 18:34-35—"In anger, his master turned him over to the jailers to be tortured, until he should pay back all he owed. This is how my heavenly Father will treat each of you unless you forgive your brother from your heart.'"

So are we forgiven by God once and for all and face no condemnation?

Or is the truth that if we fail to forgive every single person every time they do something wrong against us we face ending up in God's torture chamber?

Which is it?

Contradictions like this have gnawed at me over the years, usually subconsciously, but at times right there on the surface.

And I doubt I've been alone in this.

Not long ago I'd been working for a large corporation overseas, and with vacation time on my hands I decided it was time to take a trip to the place where it all started; where the stories of my macaroni-necklace-splattered-Sunday-School-youth were once live action theatre.

Israel.

At the time, I thought the trip had nothing to do with the theological incongruencies simmering in my subconscious through the years.

But Jerusalem had other plans.

Scene 1

Another Brick in the Wall

I was excited as I approached the security station leading to the Western Wall plaza in Jerusalem.

I was finally going to see it! The famous Wailing Wall.

As I sauntered through, bored guards fiddled with their cell phones. They paid me scant attention.

Beep-free, I emerged onto the plaza and scanned the hundreds of people milling about. People from every walk of life imaginable.

I turned toward the Wall wondering if I, a Gentile, could approach the Wall. And even more so, could I *touch* it? If for no other reason than just to say I did.

Walking toward the Wall, contrary to a sign I pass that reads, *'The Divine Presence Has Never Left the Wall,'* I believe it has. I believe the divine presence now lives in the hearts of all God's people—not figuratively, but literally.

But that's a discussion for another time. For now, I'm at the Wall.

The area of the Wall itself is cordoned off by a line of waist-high dividers. You have to walk to the far end of the plaza and down a narrow passage to actually approach the Wall. In this narrow passage, an old man stood next to a cart of yarmulkes.

"Are you Jewish?" he asked me.

My gut instinct was to answer, "Yes," and mean it. After all, I'm a card-carrying believer in every word of the Old Testament.

But I said 'no' instead. And he gave me no yarmulke.

I was allowed to approach the Wall anyway, though I remember wearing a baseball hat. Maybe he thought that was close enough.

Thinking about the whole thing later, I wish I had said 'Yes' to the question of "Are you Jewish?" because in a strange way I felt I betrayed my Jewish brothers and sisters by turning down the yarmulke. After all, it wasn't me who said 'no' as much as my cultural and religious conditioning.

'No, of course I'm not Jewish.'

But am I really *not* Jewish?

I think maybe I am. Not by ethnicity, of course, but by the fact that I'm a spiritual descendant of Abraham (Romans 4:9-17).

In that case, *Damn straight I'm Jewish...!*

When I reached out to touch the Wall, I peered at the myriad scraps of paper containing prayers, hopes, and petitions—and more than a few business cards (God, if you ever need some pipe-fitting, I'm an excellent plumber).

That's right about the time the rubber of my itchy brain met the road of my pothole-filled, always 'Under Construction' theology.

Turning to look over the masses of Orthodox Jews huddled, rocking, and gently cradling ancient scriptures in their hands, it got me thinking:

Jesus was the *Jewish* Messiah.

When the church fathers put together the canon of the Bible, at some point they made the decision to split the book into the Old and New Testaments. This was a purely arbitrary decision possibly based on the want, or need, to make a clear distinction between 'Judaism' and 'Christianity.'

At that point in history, this made perfect sense. After all, most of the New Testament deals with getting folks to understand they were now involved in a new way, a better way, a totally different way, and that going back to Old Testament religion under the Law was not only an unprofitable move, but would choke them off from the life of God (Hebrews 6 and 10).

There were great persecutions at the time of the early Christian church, and to protect this 'new way'—living solely in freedom and in God's power without religion—many people paid with their lives.

So I can see how separating the Bible to emphasize the newness and differentness of who Christ was, and what he did, made sense.

But what about us today?

Do we still have problems distinguishing Judaism from Christianity?

Probably not.

Further, maybe we've been doing ourselves a disservice by dividing the Old Testament and New Testament as it currently stands? Because under current theological structures, it seems this 'break' has caused a massive misunderstanding in how Christians, and subsequently the world, view Jesus.

Standing there at the Wall, it occurred to me: Jesus was Jewish, living in the context of Jewish culture, surrounded by Jewish people, addressing a Jewish nation.

Paul said, "But when the set time had fully come, God sent his Son, born of a woman, born under the Law..." (Galatians 4:4).

We know why Paul mentions that Jesus was born of a woman—to make clear his humanity. But why does he go out of his way to mention Jesus was born under the Law? Aren't we *all* born under the Law?

Maybe.

Maybe not.

Maybe we *aren't* all born under the Law. Maybe that's why Paul points this out about Jesus.

And this got me thinking:

Maybe it's reasonable to explore the idea that the New Testament starts with the book of Acts—the beginning of the church—rather than with the birth of Jesus?[1]

And further, what if the bulk of Jesus' words in the gospels were addressed to his culture, in *their* historical context—to those 'under the Law'—and not so much for us to live out as believers today?[2]

If this were true, how would this change our view of Jesus' 'red-letter' words?

What if the life Jesus intended for believers only makes sense *after* his death and resurrection? This would seem to clear up the clunks and clatter caused by the legalism of Jesus' words being mixed with the *freedom* Paul speaks about.

The Bible claims that the sacrifice of Jesus on the cross 2,000 years ago ended the physical and spiritual separation between God and humans that began in the Garden of Eden in Genesis 3.

Jesus was the culmination of the Law and the Old Testament sacrificial system. He was on earth to be the perfect and final sacrifice that removed forever the sin barrier separating God and humanity (refer to the entire book of Hebrews).

Even when God tried to live among humans in the Old Testament as a pillar of fire and a cloud (Deuteronomy 5:25), the sin barrier proved too much, and God retreated from the scene to await a better solution (Exodus 33-34).

Until the time of Jesus' death and resurrection, Jesus' spirit (the spirit of God) respected the barrier of sin and death erected when humanity chose to rebel. But *after* that event, God was free to come as close to his people as he could—where the two literally become one. His Spirit is now free to reside right next to ours in our inner beings.

This incredible intimacy is what God had in mind to recover since the fall of humanity in Genesis 3^3.

The Bible tells us when Jesus died, the veil of the temple (the entrance to the Holy of Holies) was torn in two (Mark 15:38). When this happened, God 'escaped' from the confines of the temple to live in and among his people in their hearts, in the innermost intimate place he could possibly be with them, for all time, forever. Never going back.

Now his people are the literal temple of God, the literal presence of God on earth (1 Corinthians 3:16; 6:19, Ephesians 2:19-22).

The Holy of Holies Gone Wild, if you will.

Isn't this incredible news?

"It is *finished,*" Jesus famously said from the cross.

So if it is finished—the fulfillment of the Law (not the abolishment of it)—where does that leave us?

It leaves us here: Jesus fulfilled the Law *so we don't have to.*

We are free to 'rest' in this intimate relationship with God, as every single thing we could ever want or need[4] is now fully taken care of by God our heavenly father, for all time.

And all this starts now, not after we 'die and go to heaven.'

So right then, in the exact moment I stood facing the Wall, I was as much a citizen of heaven as I'll ever be when my physical body passes away.

It all starts now.

———

[1] Actually, the Bible shouldn't be divided into Old Testament and New Testament at all when it gets down to it. Jesus didn't 'come out of Judaism' to start something new. I recently read a scholarly work that stated Jesus and Christianity emerged from Judaism. But is this correct? Jesus, ethnically an ancestral descendant of Isaac, was *fully* part of Judaism; the fulfillment of it. He, and Christianity, did not emerge from Judaism to start something new. His life was the fulfillment of what was there all along.

[2] This doesn't mean that Jesus didn't address the lives of future believers on a handful of occasions. He does refer a few times to people who will become believers in the future, but instead of what we've traditionally thought—that

everything he said is addressed to believers—actually only a small amount was addressed to believers. Let's keep in mind that none of the disciples were believers until after Jesus' resurrection. Even Peter, who famously answered, "You are the Messiah," was referring to Jesus as a Messiah who would overthrow the Romans physically and set up a government in Jerusalem. Thus, the swords and cutting off the ear of one of the soldiers who came to get Jesus.

[3]However, God didn't live *in* Adam and Eve, as he now does with believers after Jesus' sacrifice on the cross.

[4] We are not talking 'health and wealth gospel' here. Far from it, as you will see as we invite you to keep reading.

Scene 2

Our Flat Earth Has Always Been Round

Returning from Israel, these ideas—and some I couldn't yet articulate—wouldn't leave me alone. They grew inside me like a monstrous parasite, threatening to take over, and then...who knew? Maybe I'd explode like a fly on a windshield in line at Starbucks.

That could be messy. And costly to clean up.

I had to do something. Something drastic.

I needed to bounce these ideas off someone. They couldn't just stay in my head.

I decided it was time to call an old friend, a guy I knew since college. We'd kept in touch by phone and social media over the years I'd been abroad.

Because of work and general distractions—you know, 'life happens'—it wasn't until nine months later I was finally able to take a sabbatical from work and go back home. To the Midwestern city where I grew up.

I made the call, and my old friend agreed to meet at Boffo's Taco Grill out on 9th Street.

He arrived disheveled as ever, so I asked, "You just get up?"

D: What do you mean? It's 1:30 in the afternoon.

S: I know. You just get up?

D: Yeah.

S: Rough night?

D: What night isn't? Work, kids, you know, just living life.

S: I hear you.

D: It's been awhile, huh?

S: Yeah, maybe too long. I wanted to say thanks for meeting me. I know we have a lot to catch up on, but I want to get straight to the point. I took a trip to Israel last year and it got me thinking...a lot. I've been thinking about theology and trying to make sense of Jesus and the Bible. Kind of like we did in college when we'd stay up all night talking about life, the universe, and everything.

D: You came all the way home for that?

S: Well, I needed someone who can think outside the box without throwing out the box entirely.

D: You've piqued my interest. What's been rattling around in your head?

S: Ok, I'll just throw this out on the table: You're going to think I'm nuts, but I don't think most of Jesus' words were meant for us as believers today to try and live out. Bam. There it is.

(silence...long pause...awkward moment)

D: Hmm, well...why would you say that?

S: Follow me on this:

It seems there are two popular notions about the nature of Jesus' mission here on earth: That he came to start a new religion, and that he came to teach people how to live the Christian life.

D: That's obvious, isn't it?

S: Well, is it? That's the thing. I'm not sure either of those is correct.

D: What?

S: First, Jesus was the *Jewish* messiah, not someone coming to start a new movement or new religion.

Second, instead of Jesus' mission being to teach people how to live this new Christian life, *actually* that was the mission of the New Testament writers *after* Jesus' sacrificial death on the cross.

D: What do you think Jesus' mission actually was?

S: I think it was these two things: To fulfill the Law (Matthew 5:17) and to usher in the kingdom of God by his death and resurrection (Mark 1:15, Daniel 2:44-45).

My reasoning is the Bible tells us Jesus fulfilled the Law as the perfect sacrificial lamb (John 1:29, Hebrews 9:14). He had to live a perfect life in order to be qualified as the perfect sacrificial lamb. In doing this, living a perfect life under the Law, he showed us exactly how impossible it was for any human to do it.

And that is very important.

Secondly, by this act of his sacrifice on the cross, the physical and spiritual death-penalty for 'sin' (put into effect in Genesis 3) was destroyed forever (Romans 5). Therefore, *after* Jesus' death and resurrection, the kingdom of God has come to earth.

Jesus didn't come solely to deal with behavior (sin, fallen Adamic nature). He also came to establish and *celebrate* the fact that God lives again with his people as he did in the Garden of Eden. But this time, he doesn't just live *with* them, he lives *in* them.

D: Ok, I think I'm with you, but just to be clear: You're saying Jesus did not come to teach people how to be Christians or to live as Christians, but to show the impossibility of any human being working to be good enough to get to God on their own strength and power[1] apart from God. That it's simply impossible to attain God's standard of perfection.

S: Yes, no human can live a perfect life, but Jesus fulfilled the Law so no human has to.

D: I can see where you're going with this. And if that's true, then...

S: Then the implications on theology are vast and far reaching. Because I believe God never intended us to live Christianity as a religion.

Here's something that's been bugging me: It's common to hear people say, "There are three great monotheistic religions: Judaism, Christianity and Islam." But are they correct?

D: Yeah. Why not?

S: I think it's a false statement and always has been.

D: Why?

S: Because Christianity, as God originally intended it with Christ, is *not* a religion.[2]

Jesus, in fact, seems to be the opposite of religion; he is *anti*-religion.

If we asked Jesus his opinion on the matter, I believe he would clearly state he is unequivocally against all forms of religion (Christianity practiced as a religion included).[3] I believe he would say, "Do away with it. It's not needed. Any of it."

Recently I read a Christian blogger who realized from the variety of comments she received on her site, she seemed to have more in common with atheists than so-called Christians.

Why do you think that is?

D: Hmm. I don't know.

S; One reason might be that God's spirit is aligned with a major tenant of the atheist agenda: The eradication of all religion from the earth.

D: Whoa.

S: Shocking, isn't it? But I think Jesus would agree with the zeitgeist that religion has been one of the largest, if not *the largest,* contributor to human misery the history of the world has ever known.

Jesus said: "It is *FINISHED*" (John 19:30).

Therefore, no need for religion.

Jesus said: "I have come to set the captives free" (Luke 4:18).

Set them free from religion.

Set them free from everything.

I think Jesus took a radical departure into something completely unknown in the history of the universe: He brought freedom to humanity, not religion.

He set humanity free from religion. All religion.

D: Ok, I'm following you.

S: Consider this as well: Everyone in America, and especially we as Christian believers, often hear John 3:16 quoted.

D: "For God so loved the world, that he gave his one and only son..."

S: See? Even you can quote it. It's on TV, NFL games, everywhere. We enjoy hearing it. But the problem is we stop there.

What about Galatians 5:1? "It is for freedom that Christ has set us free." What about that as the thesis statement of the New Testament? If the gospels are actually the last four books of the Old Testament, then maybe Galatians 5:1 was always meant to be the thesis statement of the New Testament. And if that's the case, it changes everything.

D: Yes, it would.

S: I think things go further than the fact that God loved humanity so much that he sent Jesus to die on the cross for us. In Galatians 5:1, Paul says the meaning of Christ's coming was for freedom.

Freedom is the end-game.

And by stopping with John 3:16, we end up where Christian theology has been stuck for centuries, and that is, in cycles of 'trying to be good—sin/failure—repentance—go to the foot of the cross—repent—have a broken and contrite heart—pick ourselves up—go out and try again.'

How could that possibly be what Jesus intended by coming to set us free? If he didn't come to set us free from *precisely* this cycle, what exactly did he set us free from?

D: Maybe John 3:16 would be a better thesis statement for the Old Testament?

S: Not a bad idea.

D: But I have a question. If theology is not what we thought it was, should we leave it behind and head in a whole new direction, for a totally different way? Because isn't theology ancient and outdated anyway, no matter where you put the divider between the Old and New Testaments?

S: Well, actually, I don't think anything new or different is needed. Nor do I think we need to leave theology or the Bible behind. Maybe there's simply a better way to understand the words we've always been reading.

D: Like watching a 3-D movie without the glasses?

S: Something like that. Ask yourself this: When humans discovered the earth was round instead of flat, did the earth itself change when this discovery was made?

No. It was always round.

We just thought it was flat.

Same earth. Same roundness. We just came to understand it differently. But it was round the whole time.

And if there's a better, more accurate way to view theology—why wouldn't we want to go down that road? After all, it's all upside.

God should be the greatest thing we could ever

possibly know, and knowing God should mean experiencing never-ending abundant life. It seems God would constantly be revealing himself to be better than we ever thought he was, or ever could be.

So maybe it's time to get back to basics.

Or more accurately, go for the first time where nearly everyone, save for a handful of the first believing communities, have never been before.[4]

D: Ok, so if I'm following you correctly, what does it look like to move from a 'flat earth' view of Jesus to see him as he's always been?

---

[1] In the case of his specific audience, the DOI (Descendants Of Isaac) trying to 'get to God' by following the rules and rituals of the Mosaic Law.

[2] Yes, people say, "Jesus is not a religion, it's a relationship," and yes, that is correct. But it's much more than that.

[3] Let's be very clear: Jesus is not against the people who follow a religion, but he's definitely against religion as a concept.

[4] Remember that the earliest church was led entirely by the Spirit, with the aid of the Old Testament scriptures, since they did not have the New Testament scriptures yet. So when we talk of having a worldwide church led solely by the Spirit of God, am I advocating throwing out the Bible? No, not at all. We have an advantage over the early believers, in that we have the full Bible—the entire revelation of God—and we should make full use of it. We have both the Bible and the Spirit, and we should derive maximum benefit from the fact that God gave us both of these things.

Scene 3

Ordinary People

S: Did you bring a Bible with you?

D: No, but I have one in the car. I'll get it.

(*20 minutes later*)

S: Did you go to your car, or Timbuktu?

D: They don't have coffee here. I ran down to Starbucks. The line was really long.

S: Naturally.

D: You know, while I was out I thought about some of the things you were saying. If I understand you correctly, would you say one of the greatest proofs we have that the Bible is a truth set apart from all other 'religious' truths is this: That Jesus is totally unique. That Jesus is actually not a religion.

S: Yes, I would say that. This is what every New Testament writer from Acts to Revelation has been telling us for centuries: Do live in your freedom. Do not make Jesus a religion.

D: And the more we see Jesus is not a religion—and the more we live it out as a community of totally free people—the more the world, and we ourselves, will *see* God.

/thē·il·logical/ - 17

S: Yes, I think so.

D: And you came to this conclusion, not because there's a different or new way to live Christianity, but simply because our flat world has always been round. Our flat world—the fact that we did make Jesus a religion by mixing self-effort into our 'grace-oriented' relationship with God—has always been round.

S: Yes. Sounds like you got a lot of thinking done on your coffee run.

D: So how did this messed-up mixture of 'law and grace' happen? How did we miss the boat on Galatians 5:1?

S: Well, I think it happened from the historic misunderstanding that all of Jesus' words were intended for us as believers to follow and live out in our Christian lives. But actually, Jesus addressed the majority of his words only to those under the Law, *just as he was under the Law* (Galatians 4:4).

The 'red-letter' words of Jesus that sound like Law? They're just that—Law.

If we as believers live by the words of Jesus who was teaching the Law, then we are *trying to live by the Law*, and have been doing so for centuries. Which is how the mix of 'Law and grace' has infiltrated even the most grace-oriented churches.

D: But what about John 14:15, where Jesus said, "If you love me, you will obey what I command." And again in John 14:21 where he says, "Whoever has my commands and obeys them, he is the one who loves me." What about those?

S: Good question.

The answer lies in what exactly was Jesus' command

to them, and who he was addressing when he said these words. He addressed these words to his disciples and subsequently to those who would be believers after his death and resurrection. To 'obey my command' is a strong way of saying 'Do what I ask you to do.'

The question is, then, what was Jesus asking them (the disciples as a future community of believers and us) to do? In context, he's asking them to believe that God the Father and Jesus standing before them are one and the same. He's also asking them to believe that he will send them the Holy Spirit to help them, to be his literal replacement on earth, after he goes away and leaves them (dies on the cross and resurrects).[1]

D: Hmm, I'll need to think about that more.

S: Ok, but for now, I'm excited to tell you this next bit: Strap in, my friend, because we're going to see how this works practically in the Bible. Right now we're going straight into the heart of 'red-letter' Jesus with the Sermon on the Mount in Matthew 5.

D: Excellent. Let's do it.

S: First, wouldn't you agree that the Sermon on the Mount (Matthew 5-7) has been giving Christians and theologians fits for centuries about how to interpret the harsh sayings of Jesus?

D: Yes, very much so.

S: This has resulted in a theological flea market of sorts where we've picked and chosen the things we can manage, and subsequently tried to live them out, while doing a lot of theological gymnastics to get around the harsher words, such as Jesus' charge to 'be perfect' and cut off body parts 'if they cause us to sin.'

It's clear the Sermon on the Mount is impossible to live. And that was exactly what Jesus intended for us to understand in saying these things.

So I'm thinking the sayings of Jesus in the Sermon on the Mount were never meant for us as believers to follow and live out.

The New Testament from Acts to Revelation clearly urges us to live our Christian lives in freedom from rules, rituals and law (Galatians 5:1, entire book of Galatians).

D: Hmm. Again, I'll go along with it for now to see where you're going, but it'll take some time to digest.

S: Take all the time you need.

D: How about I run and get us some more coffee, to let this sink in?

S: Really? Again? Didn't you just...Ok, fine...

(time passes)

D: I'm back. Let's keep going.

S: At the start of Matthew 5, we see that Jesus is addressing the Descendants Of Isaac (DOI) only. His intent was to create a groundswell of support 'to out-Pharisee the Pharisees' (Matthew 5:20), not to pontificate to believers how to live the Christian life.

Jesus' target audience for these words has *always been* everyone who *isn't* a believer.

His intent is to show that if the DOI, or any human ever, wants to try and 'get right with God' in the power of their own moral effort apart from God (religion), the standard is perfection, which is impossible to attain by human effort (Matthew 5:48).

D: So does that mean we don't need to pay any attention to Jesus' words? What use are they to us as believers today then?

S: They're extremely useful. With these words we see that Jesus did something we could never do. He lived a perfect life under the Law.

Actually, the Sermon on the Mount is not a sermon, but a *rally*. Jesus was not preaching how to live a good and moral life. He was rallying the DOI masses to take up the challenge with him to live the Mosaic Law perfectly as God intended for them to do back in the Old Testament (Deuteronomy 5:1).

We as believers after Jesus' death and resurrection are on the sidelines *observing* this important and crucial part of Jesus' ministry.

Jesus' thoughts in Matthew chapters 5-7 are his first stand against the religion created by the DOI elite, a bastardized version of God's original intention of the Law, or what we would call 'the spirit of the Law.'

Jesus comes on the scene at a time in Israel's history when the Pharisees and Sadducees and other groups in the religious ruling power structure (a theocracy) operated under, and within, the framework of Roman puppet governors.

These religious rulers had effectively cut off—by their rules, laws, etc.—any hope of the DOI masses beneath them from 'coming to God.'

They built religious and legal structures that made them feel perfectly justified before God, while at the same time excluding everyone else from enjoying the blessings of God.

And what sickened God about this is simple: These

religious rulers gave the appearance of being 'righteous,' but they fell far short of God's true standard, which according to Jesus was absolute perfection.

Instead of God being God, they had constructed a system where God was now under their power. He was controlled by them under an elaborate system of laws and rituals—a system that was so far from what God ever intended the Law to be.

In addition to this, these religious rulers operated to the religious and financial[2] exclusion and oppression of the DOI masses and non-DOI nations around them, in direct violation of the myriad times in the Old Testament Law where God tells his people to always be hospitable to the stranger, to the visitor, to the outsider.

According to Jesus, the system the Pharisees and religious rulers had devised was characterized by hypocrisy. Because this is what religion does: It creates and breeds hypocrisy.

It *has* to.

As humans, we know instinctively in our hearts that we fall far short of God's perfect moral standard. So we make God manageable.

That's the very purpose of religion.

And it always has the effect of diminishing God's power. Because now, humans have the power and God is under our control[3]. And that is where most humans would like God to be—and stay.

The Pharisees were making it clear that anyone who wasn't as righteous as they (at least according to their system) wasn't going to make it to God. This attitude set up a caste system in Israel similar to the historic caste system in India.

The religious caste system in Israel was created during the 400 year period between the book of Nehemiah (the last dated historical book of the Old Testament) and the four gospels. This was probably a corrupted hand-me-down of Nehemiah's implorings[4] in the final chapters of his book to "see me as righteous and good before you God, separate from the underclass rabble that pays you no attention and doesn't even try to follow your Law." (*my paraphrase*)

D: That Nehemiah bit is something I've never heard before.

S: Pretty interesting, isn't it?

So Jesus enters Israel's history when the common people had no hope of ever getting to God. The religious power structure ensured that the common masses understood they were the untouchables, the outsiders.

D: That's pretty bleak.

S: Yes.

D: So how did one gain access into the elite 'in' group anyway?

S: This was how: At that time, Israel was like many countries today where your perceived skills and gifting were evaluated by your family and community at a very early age, and your future was decided based on this evaluation.

If you were the best and the brightest, you would be taken under the wing of a Rabbi, a teacher, who would 'disciple' you as their apprentice in the Law.

Eventually, if you made it through the tough years of rigorous training and religious obedience (known as the Rabbi's yoke), you just might graduate to be a Pharisee, or a member of the other powerful religious groups, yourself.[5]

This training in the Law of Moses as a disciple of a rabbi or Pharisee was your ticket to the good life, the easy life. It also, unfortunately, led to the life of a hypocrite. However, many probably started out with good intentions.

But by the time you finished your training, most were puffed-up and prideful and fully committed to make damn sure they protected their privileged status in society, and that of their newfound cronies.

D: But what about the young in Israel who weren't the best and the brightest? What about the worst and the dullest?

S: That's a good question.

Everyone in society knew that if you weren't fast-tracked by a rabbi or Pharisee, you were pretty much doomed to a life of hard labor, which most likely included poverty, and almost certainly promised a broken back and severely calloused hands in old age.

Manual labor—farming, fishing, carpentry—was your destiny and there wasn't much you could do about it.

D: That sucks.

S: Yes, it does.

At this point, it's important to note that Jesus was raised in the 'hillbilly'— or backwater—part of Israel.[6]

He was the son of a lowly carpenter, trained as a carpenter himself.

We see that when Jesus was 12-years-old, he taught and discussed the scriptures in the temple to the astonishment of the teachers and leaders (Luke 2:41-47), which most likely caused murmurs that maybe he should be fast-tracked in the Law to become a Rabbi or Pharisee himself.

D: So why didn't that happen?

S: Because that's not what God intended. God intended Jesus to be fully identified with the unwashed masses by having him born to an unmarried woman engaged to a carpenter. And for very good reason, as we shall see.

Now, though Jesus was born a backwater hick, we all know he was no ordinary carpenter.

D: Duh.

S: Through extraordinary teaching and some early miracles, Jesus quickly gained a reputation as a Rabbi, or teacher, though no one 'discipled' him or tapped him to be a Pharisee.

Jesus taught and did miracles solely by God's authority and the fact that John the Baptist and God himself picked him at his baptism (Mark 1:9-11).

S: You following me so far?

D: Got it.

S: So now we're at the stage where Jesus is approximately 30 years old, and beginning what is now known as his public ministry.

One of the first things Jesus did in his public ministry as a Rabbi was pick disciples. But instead of choosing the best and the brightest, he chose the ordinaries and the dullards. Not that they were actually ordinary and dull—that was simply how society had labeled the circumstances of their births.

But Jesus saw more in them.

Jesus saw that the men he chose as his disciples[7] fit perfectly with God's purposes. They had abilities perfect for their eventual destinies.

Jesus valued in them what everyone else had overlooked. When Jesus chose these men, they saw themselves exactly as society painted them. But God was about to change all that. As he still does in billions of lives to this day.

D: Excellent background.

S: Thanks.

D: And now the Sermon on the Mount?

S: Coming right up.

---

[1] He also asks later, in a statement addressed to believers who will be around after his death, to go to the ends of earth and spread the good news (Matthew 28:18-20), but this is to be done after they have waited for the Holy Spirit to come and initiate the action (Acts 1:4).

[2] As evidenced by the temple clearing and money changer-whippings.

[3] Sound familiar? 'You will be like God' (Genesis 3:4-5).

[4] Do Nehemiah's words sound familiar? Check out Luke 18:9-14.

[5] Each of the religious ruling groups had a slightly different twist on the main goal of life, and how to solve the particular problems faced by the DOI at this time, being shackled under an occupying country and army—the Romans. The

Pharisees' outlook on life was to follow the Law of God to perfection, and that would solve all problems. Well, as they saw 'perfection' anyway. But in their defense, truly following the Law was their stated 'outward' goal as a group.

[6] The region around the Sea of Galilee is economically depressed to this day. Fishing was then, and is now—along with tourism—still the main economic driver of the region.

[7] As a kid growing up in America, I always wondered why Jesus' disciples 'immediately dropped everything' and followed him. They didn't even seem to know the guy, yet they just threw down everything and entrusted their entire lives to him. How weird. But now I realize they immediately left their current lives because they were being handed an opportunity to fast-track themselves to the easy privileged life, and they were under no circumstances going to jeopardize it by dilly-dallying. After all, the rabbi is asking now, and if they dilly-dally, he might just go and pick someone else. So they dropped everything—literally dropped their fishing nets—and followed him.

Scene 4

So This Blind Man With No Arms and No Legs Walks Into a Bar...

S: Let's turn to Matthew chapter 5 and dig into the Sermon on the Mount.

D: I'm ready.

S: Let's rock.

D: Wait a minute. Let's not rock...yet. I want to get another cup of coffee. And while I'm gone, I'll consider whether or not you're certifiably insane.

S: Whatever floats your boat.

(time passes)

S: You ready now?

D: Let's rock.

S: So one fine day Jesus gathers his small band of disciples and some common people on an ordinary hill in a backwater area of Israel called Galilee.

These people were the commoners, the hillbillies, the underclasses, and despised of Israel. "Can anything good come from Nazareth?" one man condescendingly remarked in John 1:46.

But the unwashed masses started following Jesus around the countryside because of his growing reputation as a miracle worker and an authority in the Law.

D: Wait a minute. Did you insinuate earlier that Jesus was a hick?

S: Yes.

D: Why do you say that?

S: Well, besides the underclass circumstance of his birth, the Bible tells us Jesus was not impressive or anything great to look at (Isaiah 53:2). Jesus was not a rock star or a Bollywood celebrity.

D: Hmm. I can see that. But I've been to Europe and seen paintings of him with that Bon Jovi hair.

S: Yeah, well, I don't think that was his real...

D: Just kidding. Keep going.

S: Ok. With everyone gathered on this hill in Galilee, Jesus gave a prelude to his rally of the people with a vignette popularly known today as the 'Beatitudes.'

D: I love the Beatitudes.

S: With the Beatitudes, Jesus contrasted what was valued in God's kingdom with what was valued in the Roman kingdom. Rome valued conquering strength, military might and set apart for greatness those who exuded those qualities. In contrast, God valued peace, the common everyday person, and those who pursued justice (Matthew 5:1-12).

After this warm-up, after everyone was sufficiently

knocked off balance a bit, Jesus told the crowd, in effect, "Now we're going to storm the castle! We're going to *out Pharisee the Pharisees*!"

And the people loved it! They were ready. "Yes, yes!" they must have told Jesus, "Show us how!"

The masses knew 'the system.' They knew what it meant to 'get to God' by the Law.

So Jesus' first mission was to show the world *exactly* what it would look like, what you would *actually* have to do, to 'get to God' by living the Law.

And there was only one way to do it: By living an absolutely perfect life.

Perfect.

Meaning you never did anything against God's character. Ever.

Never. Ever. Ever. Ever.

At any moment of your entire life.

Ever.

Perfect.

Perfection.

That was what was required.

And anything less, one smallest of missteps, and you're 'out.' Hell awaits.

That is the standard of 'getting to God' by the Law.

D: So what you're saying is, that in essence, almost every red-letter thing Jesus says in Matthew could be prefaced with this: "If you want to make things right between you and God by using the Law (your own religious and moral efforts apart from the power of God), this is what it looks like..."

S: Exactly. You got it.

But the common rabble were thinking something very different from what Jesus had in mind about the Law.

They were thinking what it meant to 'be perfect' was reflected in the way of life of the Pharisees. And of course, the Pharisees held that their version of following the Law was adequate for all matters between man and God.

Which brings us to the thesis statement of the book of Matthew; Matthew 5:17, where Jesus says, "I have not come to abolish the law, but to fulfill it."

In case anyone on that hill thought Jesus was teaching and preaching a 'new' Law by the extremes of what he said, Jesus clarified: "No, I'm not talking about the eradication of the Mosaic Law for a 'new Law.' What I'm talking about is what it means to actually live by, and fulfill, the Mosaic Law. The same Law everyone, including and especially the Pharisees, are trying to follow now."

So Jesus starts out his rallying speech with, "You are to be the salt of the earth..."

And the people probably thought, "Yes, we are! We can do that!"

"...but if the salt loses its saltiness...it is no longer good for anything, except to be thrown out and trampled by men."

"Eek! Ouch, hmmmm, well..."

Then he said, "We are going to be a city on a hill, shining brightly for the whole world to see..."[1]

"Yes! We can do that! Awesome! We're ready!"

"The surrounding nations are going to see your good deeds (your moral superiority) and be drawn to God..."

"Yes, they will! We can do it!"

"And this is how: We're going to strictly follow the Law of Moses as God originally intended it" (Matthew 5:17-18)

"Uh...ok...I suppose so...Yes! We're ready!"

"And anyone who breaks one of the least of these commandments and teaches others to do the same, will be *least* in the kingdom of heaven, but whoever follows them perfectly will be called greatest in the kingdom of heaven" (Matthew 5:19).

"Uh, that's kind of harsh... but, uh, ok, we can be good enough....We will do it! If the Pharisees can do it, so can we!"

Then Jesus appeals to their pride in 'wanting' to follow the Law. They *want* to be known as being good enough. They *want* to be a 'city on a hill,' a 'righteous beacon' shinning for all the 'unrighteous nations (the dogs[2]).' They want to be the envy of other nations who were destined to be judged by God as not being good and perfect like the shinning DOI.

Jesus was handing them a great deal! Or so they thought.

"Your righteousness must surpass that of the Pharisees..." (vs. 20).

"Yes! Yes! We'll show them we can do it! We'll show

them who's boss!"

"Make sure you've done everything to make everything right with everyone around you before you find yourself before God and he finds 'sins' that are still outstanding. Remember, you must be perfect when you stand before God" (vs. 21-26).

"Um...yeah...got it. Can do! We're with you...but, um, everything? Hmmm...*everything*?"

"If a body part causes you to sin, cut it off—arms, eyes, what-have-you! Better to lose a body part than be thrown into Hell with your body intact!" (vs. 27-30)

"*Are you kidding? WHAT THE HELL?*"

"Let's not pretend that this is easier than it really is" (vs. 29, MSG).

"Ha! What? Did he really just say that?....*Really?*"

"You heard 'eye for an eye' under Moses. But I say, when someone attacks you, just take it. Do whatever is necessary to not fight back. Ever" (vs. 38-39).

"Oooooooooh...wow...not sure if we can do that..."

"Always go the extra mile for everyone, especially someone taking unfair advantage of you. Do a lot more for every single person you run into than they expect of you, and more than you even expect of yourself..." (vs. 40-42).

"Dang it! I can't do that! Can you imagine what it would take to do that? *Is this guy crazy?*"

"Love your enemies..." (vs. 43).

"*WHAT?* Even the *Romans?*"

By saying this, Jesus was asking the masses, "Can you match the character of God? Can you be *that* perfect?"

Then he lowers the ultimate boom:

Matthew 5:48: "Be <u>*perfect*</u>, as your heavenly father is perfect."

"THAT'S IMPOSSIBLE!"

But there it is.

The *truth* and the *challenge*.

If you want to get to God on the basis of your own merits apart from God, then you must be perfect.

If you stand alone before God and expect to be considered 'acceptable' in the presence of the absolute perfect creator and owner of the universe, then *you must also be perfect.*

That is what is required.

This should have harkened them back to Adam and Eve in the Garden of Eden who rebelled against God because they wanted to be like God (Genesis 3:5).

So what is required for humans to be brought back into God's presence? Perfection; being like God.

Through Jesus' words, God is lovingly saying, "Ok, you wanted to be like me—so how's that working out for you? Can you be perfect, just like me?"

And it's not that God is being a dick. It's just that God's perfect nature cannot stand the presence of human 'sin' nature. Corrupt human nature simply cannot mix with the perfect divine nature without God's presence killing them (Isaiah 6:5), in the same way we cannot live under water without it killing us.

It's not that we or the water is being a jerk and decided that we or the water does or doesn't want to do it.

No. It's that it can't be done, according to the laws of science and nature.

It has nothing to do with our wills, or the will of the water. It's not a matter of what either party wants or doesn't want.

It simply can't be done.

Same with humans and God when the 'sin' barrier of the original rebellion of humans (Genesis 3) is still intact.

D: Hmm. That's interesting. Keep going.

S: So there it is, straight from Jesus' mouth: We cannot live in the presence of a perfect God without being perfect ourselves. That's just the way it is. As it should be. Because would we want the God of the universe to be anything less than perfect? I would think not.[3]

So in conclusion to Matthew 5, as believers today we must seriously ask ourselves: Is Jesus inviting us into the way of life described so far in the Sermon on the Mount?

Is Jesus inviting us, commanding us, to strive to get to God in our own moral effort by the Law apart from God?

I think not.

Jesus was actually describing his life—what he was going to do to fulfill the Law. And in this rallying speech on the side of an obscure, backwater Galilean hill, he invited anyone who wanted to 'try' to be perfect to come right along with him.

He invited them: "Let's see if you can do it."

And in retrospect, after his resurrection, his followers would have understood all of this in that context.

We, as believers after his death and resurrection, have been set free (Galatians 5:1).

But wait! Houston, we have a problem! Traditionally, the Sermon on the Mount continues for two more chapters of Jesus teaching Law to those under the Law (Matthew 6-7).

But is this correct?

Or does Jesus teach Law to those under the Law for nearly the entire book of Matthew?

D: I can't wait to find out.

---

[1] Considering that Jesus was not referring to us as believers with these statements, the children's song "This little light of mine. I'm gonna let it shine...," strikes me as being a very odd song. Jesus was speaking of the DOI as being God's representative nation on earth, a light, a beacon of moral goodness to the surrounding nations. He was not referring to us as Christians being 'lights' in the world. To a person standing on that hillside, excitement would crackle through the crowd because Jesus was rallying the DOI to the glory days of David and Solomon. That as God's chosen people, the y were a moral light to the nations, a city on a hill. This Mosaic Law concept was never intended to go forward after Jesus rose from the dead. After Jesus rose, this concept was 'finished.'

[2] Mark 7:26-30

[3] Well, technically, we do want our god(s) to be less than perfect, because that makes them manageable and controllable for us, and therefore easy to manipulate. This is what the Bible calls 'idols.' But God's thoughts on that is "Why would you want a god that is powerless to help you and powerless to take care of you and provide for you? Don't you want the real thing?" And we are free to choose exactly that—the real thing, or a fake.

Scene 5

...And Says, "Excuse Me, Gotta Drink For a Man on His Way to Heaven?"

S: At the beginning of Matthew 6, Jesus continues his Sermon on the Mount statements of how to live a perfect life under the Law.

D: Not for us as believers today to live out and follow?

S: Correct, not for us.

So in Matthew 6:9, we come to the famous 'Lord's Prayer.'

D: I love the Lord's Prayer. Don't mess with the Lord's Prayer, man.

S: I'm not going to mess with it. I just want to take the line of reasoning we've been following and apply it to The Lord's Prayer, to consider the possibility it wasn't meant for us as believers.

D: Not for us? Are you crazy? It's read and recited in churches every Sunday, and has been for centuries...

S: I know, but I'm not sure Jesus was teaching us how to pray. I think he was teaching the DOI how to pray under the perfection that the Law requires.

D: Umm, ok. I guess I can see that in context.

S: It's very important to stay in context when interpreting scripture. So in light of context, does it make sense for us to recite this prayer each week in church, or even to use this as a model for how we are to pray?

D: It seems not.

S: Exactly.

Galatians 3 is clear that we as believers are to live by the Spirit.

And if we live by the Spirit, there are no models. There is only freedom. The freedom of resting in our inner-spirits (Matthew 11:28-30)[1] and allowing the life of the living, infinite and unpredictable Spirit of God—who is always good and loving and just—to act in us and through us to love those around us.

Since as believers we live in an intimate freedom-based relationship with God, no models are needed to be followed for prayer, or anything else in our relationship with God.

When it comes to prayer, we pray in conversation with God just as we would talk to a family member or friend. After all, hasn't God gone out of his way to show he's our heavenly father, and doesn't Paul tell us in 2 Corinthians 5 to 'be a friend of God'?

D: I'll look it up, but yes, I think so.

S: What this means is there is an infinitely complex number of 'prayer models' (no longer models, but conversations), since there is an infinite number of complex humans created and loved by God.

And that sounds pretty damn good to me.

D: Me too.

S: In addition to the 'Lord's Prayer' being a model for how to pray under the Law, I think Jesus was urging the DOI to be prayerfully aware of what was coming; what was about to be fulfilled.

Jesus was telling them to have eyes to see it. Have ears to hear it. Look forward to it with awe and reverence.

Jesus was saying what happens in heaven will soon be happening on earth as well. God's kingdom will be reinstated on earth to exist side by side for a time with the 'human kingdom (which includes the powers of spiritual darkness)' (Matthew 13:1-9; 18-23; 36-43).

What's coming when God's kingdom arrives involves the forgiveness of sins. What's coming is a reinstatement of the Garden of Eden economy, where God promises to provide for all our needs.

It seems reciting the Lord's Prayer on a regular basis in church or Christian gatherings would be like standing up at the beginning of history class today and reciting Thomas Paine's *Common Sense* with the expectation of its fulfillment now and in the future, instead of realizing its significance lies solely in the historical past.[2]

The war between England and the American colonies has been settled.

With Jesus' death and resurrection, the war between God and Satan's forces has been settled.

This doesn't mean *Common Sense* should be thrown out and no longer studied. Far from it. Its value to us now is that we see it in the context of its historical fulfillment.

With the Lord's Prayer, Jesus, like Babe Ruth, pointed

to the right field wall and predicted a homerun. "Watch, I'm about to knock one outta the park..."

D; Nice analogy.

S: Thanks. But if we're still not convinced that the Lord's Prayer is not for us, then this should put the nail in the coffin: The fact that people stop at verse 13 and fail to go on to verse 14.

Verse 14 starts with a 'For,' which can also be translated 'therefore.' A 'therefore' means what comes next is based on what was just said. In this case, Jesus says the Lord's Prayer, then says what the audience is supposed to do about it.

And here it is: Matthew 6:14: "For if you forgive other people when they sin against you, your heavenly Father will also forgive you. But if you do not forgive others their sins, your Father will not forgive your sins."

D: Whoa! Has that really been there all along?

S: Yes. And that's what's so interesting. Verse 14 was always meant to go with the Lord's Prayer. And verse 14 contains the conditional nature of the Mosaic Law: If you do 'X,' God will bless you. If you don't do 'X,' you get judgment and condemnation. So verse 14 and the Lord's Prayer is clearly Jesus teaching the Mosaic Law to those under the Law.

D: Ok, that's pretty clear. I like what you're saying, but again I have to ask: If we throw out the Lord's Prayer and the Sermon on the Mount as something believers aren't supposed to do and follow today, then what are we to make of Jesus' words? Pay no attention to them at all?

S: These words of Jesus are extremely valuable, just not in the way we thought they were.

Look at the Sermon on the Mount. Jesus said that is what it takes to be 'perfect' before God.

Today we can be extremely grateful that Jesus has fulfilled the Law so no human has to.

No one has to cut off body parts.

Why?

Because Jesus fulfilled the Law.

Paul in the New Testament is constantly cultivating an attitude of thankfulness toward God. We can thank God for our freedom in Christ and be happy about what he did for us on the cross.

D: And because of that gratitude, we should *do* things for God; work for God, serve him, show our appreciation for what he did. Right?

S: Well, that's what I hear in a lot of churches, but no, I don't think that's the response we should have.

D: What do you mean? Sure it is. I'm grateful for what Jesus did for me, so I want to serve God in return out of gratitude. What could be wrong with that?

S: Paul says if we have that response we're once again shackling ourselves to the very thing from which Christ set us free (book of Galatians).

Jesus set us free from living under laws and rules and 'working' for God—even from cycles of sin-confession-repentance-grace at the foot of the cross-try again as we go along in a process of 'sanctification.'

The Christian life is actually none of that, according to Galatians 5:1.

D: Wow, you're spinning my gears, man.

S: Yeah, but isn't it great? Who doesn't like freedom and more freedom?

D: I'd love more freedom...you know, I thought it was weird when you called me out of the blue and wanted to talk about this. But now I know why you did. Because I needed to hear it. Years ago, when I first heard about Jesus, it was new and fresh; I couldn't get enough of it. But now, I wouldn't wish the Christian life on my own worst enemy.

S: Oh? Why is that?

D: Because if God is really there and loving, what I was doing just didn't quite line up with what I thought was true about God. Where was the 'abundant life' Jesus promised? Everything I was doing seemed a far cry from "Come to me, all who are burdened and heavy laden, and I will give you rest." It seemed like the opposite.

I was burned-out and exhausted, endlessly adding more to my "To Do" list for God.

So one day I just sat down and thought, is this really what it's all about? Doing all this stuff for God?

Since then, I've had this subconscious gnawing that maybe I wasn't seeing things right. I just couldn't quite put my finger on what I was missing.

S: I'm sad to hear that's been your experience. But it was mine too, in many ways.

But you know, it's good for us to come to the end of our rope. Jesus did say, "You're blessed when you come to the end of your rope. With less of you, there is more of God and his rule" (Matt 5:3[3], MSG).

It means that if we just step back and stop striving, we'll *see* God.

D: I like the verse "Quit striving and know that I am God" (Psalm 46:10).

S: Yes, exactly.

The life God meant for us is not one of constant striving to 'perfect' ourselves, or always striving to stay in 'God's good graces' so he doesn't turn his back on us.

Ours wasn't meant to be a life of striving at all, but one of rest and freedom and seeing God. Participating and partnering with him as he reveals himself and his plans. We wait for God to act, then we join in what he is doing. The trick is getting ourselves out of the way so we can see him. That's when life is exciting. That's when we experience abundant life.

D: Can you give some examples of that?

S: There are some great ones in the book of Acts—Peter and Cornelius, Peter and the sick man on the way to the temple, Peter speaking at Pentecost. All of these things were God-initiated events, not man-initiated events. Peter simply joined in what God was doing.

D: All right. I really like where this is going. But I'm supposed to meet my brother in a couple hours at Jimmy Picaya's Lobster Barn. Have you ever been there? It's a nice place. Food's great.

S: Never heard of it. But I've been out of the country a

few years.

D: I'll call and reschedule with him for tomorrow night. I'd like to keep talking.

S: Are you sure?

D: Yeah.

S: Tell him I said hi.

---

[1] The Sabbath day Old Testament law (a weekly rest day from work) foreshadowed that we now rest spiritually in God all the time after the death and resurrection of Jesus. Under the Mosaic Law, keeping the Sabbath was about physical work and rest. Now it's about spiritual rest in our inner beings. It's interesting to note that as Christians and Gentiles, we were never meant to follow the 613 Mosaic laws. The book of Hebrews explains this very clearly. Only the DOI were 'under the Law contract' with God to follow the Law. Why does this matter? Why not let someone live by the laws of God if they want? Well, true, in your freedom in Christ, you are free to follow the Mosaic Law. But Paul calls that foolishness; it does more harm than good. The Oscar winning movie *Chariots of Fire* depicts the true story of an Olympic runner who struggled, and damn near gave up his Olympic dreams, because he didn't read Hebrews closely enough. He thought the Old Testament law pertaining to the Sabbath (one of the Ten Commandments) applied to him; that God wants us as believers after Christ's resurrection to physically rest one day a week without doing any work. Eric Liddell considered running in his Olympic races to be 'work.' Poor guy. So instead of this being a movie about a triumph of faith and respect for God, actually it's an excruciatingly tragic hour-and-a-half of needless, soul-wrenching suffering. It's horrible. Eric Liddell was totally free in Christ, but chose to enslave himself to a law that not only no longer applied to him, but never applied to him as a Gentile in the first place, simply because he didn't grasp Galatians, Hebrews and the rest of the New Testament. The second half of Galatians 5:1 says to everyone free in Christ, "Never again let anyone put a

harness of slavery on you." (MSG) So...Oscar winning drama? Nope. Oscar winning tragedy? Yes.

² Further, if England had won the war, we might not be aware today that *Common Sense* ever existed, much less celebrate its meaning. It would have been relegated to the historical infamy of *Mein Kampf.* And if Jesus hadn't won the war in the spiritual realm, we wouldn't have the gospel accounts at all. So even more was at stake in Jesus' day.

³ The Beatitudes were not part of the Mosaic Law. They were wisdom sayings, a warm-up act before Jesus launched into teaching the Law. Also, under Roman rule, blessings went to those who were strongest, most militant and violent in pursuit of 'peace' and the preservation of the Roman Empire. Jesus turns this ideology on its head. God's kingdom, God's economy, does not work that way

Scene 6

Walking the Spiritual Plank

D: So where are we?

S: Matthew 6:16:

> When you fast, do not look somber as the hypocrites do, for they disfigure their faces to show others they are fasting. Truly I tell you, they have received their reward in full. But when you fast, put oil on your head and wash your face, so that it will not be obvious to others that you are fasting, but only to your Father, who is unseen; and your Father, who sees what is done in secret, will reward you. (Matthew 6:16)

This passage talks about fasting. But again, in context of Jesus teaching the Law to those under the Law, I don't think these words were meant for believers today.

This being the case, Jesus does not ask or require *us* to fast.

Of course, if we feel led by the Spirit to fast in God's strength and power, then by all means, we're free to do so. But we can't judge those who don't, or make them feel like they should, or worse, make them feel any less of a member of God's family because in their freedom they choose not to fast, and never do, just as in your freedom, you may fast if you want.[1]

D: I tried to fast once. I was really hungry. But some

say it can be good for your health.

S: I've heard that, too. And the great thing about living in freedom by the Spirit is that we can practice spiritual and physical disciplines all day long if we want to. Or not.[2]

Ok, let's keep going and see what else we're not mandated to do:

Matthew 6:19, the famous 'treasures in heaven' passage:

> Do not store up for yourselves treasures on earth, where moths and vermin destroy, and where thieves break in and steal. But store up for yourselves treasures in heaven, where moths and vermin do not destroy, and where thieves do not break in and steal. For where your treasure is, there your heart will be also. (Matthew 6:19)

Again, beautiful passage, beautiful words, but not meant for us to live out. It's part of being 'perfect' under the Law.

With these verses, Jesus is telling the DOI to follow the 'path to God' perfectly with full and undistracted concentration.

"Don't look at what you gather on earth to be most important," Jesus tells them. What is most important in getting to God in your own moral strength apart from God is focusing wholeheartedly on what will bring you 'treasures in heaven.'

And you'll only get them by perfection.

If we think this passage is about 'rewards' Christians will one day gain for our service to God, then we live the Christian life as a religion; far from freedom (Galatians 5:1) and rest (Matthew 11:28-30).

The context of the 'treasures in heaven' passage is still perfection under the Law.

Human nature, according to Jesus in Matthew 6:22-25, is not neutral. Humans don't merely choose to do right or wrong. We have no choice in the matter. We do wrong because human nature is bent away from God. We can't help it. We can't steer it.

But yes, we can put a Band-Aid on a shotgun wound if we want to (religion). But ultimately there's nothing we can do to change our inner-most natures. And Jesus says there needs to be a wholesale change of our inner-nature, not just managing good and bad behavior on the outside (religion).

This point is what the Pharisees failed to understand. That ultimately what is needed is a change of our very nature.

Trying to be morally good before God always falls short. And thinking you are 'ok' because you've lessened the requirements of God (hypocrisy) is what the Pharisees were doing.

Jesus said living like that is of no use. It's bunk. It won't get you where you want to go.

Continuing on, we see in Matthew 6:25-34 that part of what it means to be perfect before God is not worrying, because worry is the opposite of trust that God will take care of you.

> "Therefore I tell you, do not worry about your life, what you will eat or drink; or about your body, what you will wear. Is not life more than food, and the body more than clothes? Look at the birds of the air; they do not sow or reap or store away in barns, and yet your heavenly Father feeds them. Are you not much more valuable than they? Can any one of you by worrying add a single hour to your life?

"And why do you worry about clothes? See how the flowers of the field grow. They do not labor or spin. Yet I tell you that not even Solomon in all his splendor was dressed like one of these. If that is how God clothes the grass of the field, which is here today and tomorrow is thrown into the fire, will he not much more clothe you—you of little faith? So do not worry, saying, 'What shall we eat?' or 'What shall we drink?' or 'What shall we wear?' For the pagans run after all these things, and your heavenly Father knows that you need them. But seek first his kingdom and his righteousness, and all these things will be given to you as well. Therefore do not worry about tomorrow, for tomorrow will worry about itself. Each day has enough trouble of its own." (Matthew 6:25-34)

Jesus says that trusting God to fully provide for your needs is a requirement of the Law. You must have perfect faith and trust in God to go along with your perfect moral lives.

It's important to note here that Jesus is saying 'do not worry' for a completely different reason, in a completely different context, than urgings of 'Do not worry' as seen in Philippians, James and other New Testament books.

Jesus, and the DOI, were under the covenant of the Mosaic Law. And under that covenant, God's blessings were contingent upon the DOI following the Law in perfect faith. If you did that, you got blessings. If you didn't, you got curses. This is reiterated throughout the whole Old Testament.

In other words, under the Law, if your behavior shows you don't trust God, you're in danger of curses.

James and Paul, however, urge Christians not to worry because after Jesus' death and resurrection, all has been finished by God.

All has been reconciled between God and humans, so rest and live in freedom. No need to worry. Don't stress yourselves out. God promises to take care of you no matter what.

God fulfilling his promise to take care of you is sealed by the Spirit in you, and he'll never abandon himself, ever (2 Timothy 2:13). God taking care of you is not contingent on your actions, attitude or behavior. Ever.

And that's freedom.

S: Can you see the difference?

D: Yes. I like it. It's making sense.

S: Excellent. Let's continue.

In Matthew 6:33, Jesus told the masses "Seek first God's kingdom and his righteousness, and all these things will be added to you as well."

In other words, he was charging them to focus wholeheartedly and undistractedly on God's kingdom and all their needs would be met. Again, he was reiterating the terms of the Mosaic Law contract.

And, again, if we do this as Christians today, we are merely trying to follow the Law in our own effort, which is religion.

D: In my earlier Christian life, I used this passage, "Seek first the kingdom of God, and all these things will be added to you" as a mantra. I even tacked it above the doorway of my house to remind me before I went out. But it was a mantra that failed. For some reason, I always felt burned-out and exhausted.

S: It should have exhausted you if you were trying to follow it. Because that's Law, that's religion.

D: Ok, I can see that now. If you want to get to God in your own power, then be perfect, seek his kingdom, seek his righteousness, "Be perfect as your Father in heaven is perfect," and you will be blessed—all these things will be added to you.

S: Yes. You do 'X' for God and he'll do 'Y' for you. But none of this is for us. Ephesians 2:6 tells us as believers we're seated with Christ in heaven *right now*.

Can anything be added to that?

Paul tells us in the first chapter of Ephesians, now that you've been fully identified with Christ in his death and resurrection (Galatians 2:20), therefore, everything that belongs to Christ is yours. Everything that is true of Christ, is true of you.

Everything.

Because we are God's adopted children.

We have access to everything God has, which is everything.

D: That's pretty all-inclusive if you ask me.

S: I think so. Ok, going on to Matthew 7, we see that part of perfection under the Law is not judging others:

> "Do not judge, or you too will be judged. For in the same way you judge others, you will be judged, and with the measure you use, it will be measured to you. Why do you look at the speck of sawdust in your brother's eye and pay no attention to the plank in your own eye? How can you say to your brother, 'Let me take the speck out of your eye,' when all the time there is a plank in your own eye? You hypocrite, first take the plank out of your own eye, and then you will see clearly to remove the speck from your brother's eye." (Matthew 7:1-5)

We've commonly heard that the plank in the eye

statement is for *us* as Christians. That we should not be hypocrites with one another. But again, this statement was not meant for us, nor is the 'spirit' or 'truthfulness' of the statement meant for us either.

Jesus is calling out the hypocrisy of the Pharisees. He's publically exposing their hypocrisy, because they are under the Law.

So this passage does not expose *our* hypocrisy, or teach us not to be hypocrites with fellow believers (or anyone for that matter) because we are not under the Law (see Romans 5-8, and the entire book of Hebrews).

In that regard, it makes no sense to apply this scenario to *us*.

It's illogical.

D: But it's still bad to judge each other, right?

S: Well, yes, we know it's not loving to judge each other. But we are not to bother ourselves with planks and logs and running around sifting individual behaviors.

We live in freedom in the Spirit (Galatians 5:1, Galatians 5:18), and if we have to confront someone for their bad behavior towards ourselves or others, it's perfectly ok to confront them even if we are the biggest sinner in the world and they have done something relatively small.

Because we're not playing a game of 'one-upmanship' in behavior.

We are playing a game of love.

And in love, it's perfectly fine for a murderer to confront a gossip.

Because the gossip benefits by being shown the path back to freedom and love regardless of the behavior of the murderer.

And the Spirit is always looking to do what benefits others regardless of our current status. That is the constant outward focus that characterizes the very nature of God.

To reiterate the overall point, as Christians, we are not to be involved in rule-keeping and law, with ourselves or others. We are to have nothing to do with keeping score with regards to sin.

Neither are we to have anything to do with planks and logs and eyes with planks and logs in them.

D: So I have to ask again, though, what is the value of these words being in the Bible at all if it's not for us?

S: The value is tremendous!

We can thank God we are *free* and not under Law, therefore we don't have to bother with planks and logs and eyes.

Another value is that we can see what happens if we're tempted to fall back into 'religion'—turning our backs on Jesus + Nothing—as warned against in Hebrews chapters 6 and 10.

D: I think I see it now. If I were in the Pharisees shoes—if I were trying to get to God by the Law—it would lead me to constantly compare my behavior with others.

S: That's right. 'Religion' only leads to planks and logs and eyes and hypocrisy and slavery to keeping score with sin. We've been rescued from all that to live a brand new way under a new covenant.

Remember, the record of Jesus' life (the gospels) is the final act of the Old Testament, not the first act of the New Testament.

Jesus continues to teach the Law to those under the Law in Matthew 7:7—"This is how you live in relation to God under the Law: Seek and you will find, knock and the door will be opened to you." (*my paraphrase*)

If you are living perfectly in perfect relationship to God under the Law, God will provide you with everything. Again, these are the terms of the Mosaic Law contract—do the right thing, and be blessed; do the wrong thing, and suffer curses.

Jesus sums up all these seemingly nice and innocent statements about Law in Matthew 7:12: This is the summation of the law: "So in everything, do to others what you would have them do to you, for this sums up the Law and Prophets."

This is not a suggestion by Jesus, or a mantra to live by, or a 'golden rule' to guide us as humans or as Christians.

No.

Jesus is spelling out exactly what it looks like if anyone chooses to try to live a perfect life under the Law in order to get 'right with God' in their own efforts apart from God, which is religion.

Any religion.

Buddhism, Islam, Mormonism, Judaism, Jehovah's Witnesses, Animism, Voodoo, Baha'i, Kabala, Hinduism, including Christianity as a religion.

All religions.

All religions fall short.

Because they do not allow adherents to live in freedom. The devout are shackled in slavery to laws, rules and rituals, appeasing gods and spirits and managing their own behavior.

Shackled.

When Jesus says, "In everything, do unto others as you would have them do unto you," he is teaching Law to the DOI, and he actually means in *everything*.

EVERY.

THING.

Do to others as you would have them do to you.

Not in most things. Or as many as you can manage.

But in everything.

Perfection.

And when his audience heard this, they would've been thinking, 'But...but....*EVERYTHING*? Whew! That's a tall order. But that's...that's.....IMPOSSIBLE!'

This reaction is exactly what Jesus wanted to elicit from his audience, then and now.

This is exactly the conclusion Jesus wants everyone in the world to come to.

All humans.

Everywhere.

For all time.

That if you think you can get to God by your religious moral efforts, rituals, and good behavior apart from

God, then be warned—it's impossible.

And worse, it's shackling. It's an enslaved way to live.

Which brings us to one of the most famous passages in the Bible.

And in keeping in the flow and context of what we've been discussing, a more accurate interpretation of this passage could possibly cause us to stand back in awe of the greatness and power of God.

---

[1] This goes for the relatively recent (in Christian history) new rules we impose on ourselves and others of daily Bible reading, serving others, and/or a regular 'quiet time.' If you want to do a quiet time, you are free to do so. If you don't want to, you are free not to. But you are certainly not free to judge those who in their freedom choose not to. But, you say, it's a means of growth? How will we grow without spiritual disciplines? The answer: you are right now in this moment fully identified with Christ. What do you need to grow into? Jesus is God. Jesus is perfection. And he lives in and through you right now (Galatians 2:20).

[2] There are many disciplines that are good for us, but they're only for our personal benefit and the benefit of others around us. They don't affect our 'standing' with God. He has everything and he's fine. Quiet times, Bible study, contemplative prayers and meditations, service to others, accountability groups and any and all other valid Christian disciplines are important. But if they become a system to measure how we are 'doing' with God, or worse, how we measure others' progress with God, then we're missing the mark. Christian disciplines are healthy if we keep them in correct perspective.

Scene 7

The Narrow Road *Never* Traveled

S: Ok, keeping in mind we're still deep in the Sermon on the Mount—Jesus teaching Law to those under the Law—let's consider this famous passage of scripture:

> "Enter through the narrow gate. For wide is the gate and broad is the road that leads to destruction, and many enter through it. But small is the gate and narrow is the road that leads to life, and only a few find it." (Matthew 7:13-14)

In context, the *narrow gate* is perfection under the Law; Jesus' goal with the Sermon on the Mount.

D: What did you say?

S: The narrow gate is perfection under the Law.

The broad road that leads to destruction is where everyone finds themselves who fails to live an absolutely perfect life under the Mosaic Law.

And entering the narrow gate (perfection) that leads to God's life—getting right with God, entering God's life, entering God's kingdom by your own merits and moral perfection apart from God—is something *few* will find.

D: Are you sure that's a more accurate interpretation?

S: I think so.

We all know the traditional interpretation of this

passage, that Jesus equated himself with "the narrow gate that leads to life," something only a few will find.

Which has led many to conclude that Jesus is saying few will enter God's kingdom (go to Heaven when they die), but the majority of humans, who are on the wide road to destruction, will end up in Hell.

But I think a more accurate interpretation is that Jesus is equating the narrow gate with perfection under the Law in our own efforts apart from God, and facetiously states that no one will get into God's kingdom (Heaven) that way.

Because it's impossible.

Jesus uses the device of understatement with the phrase, "few will find it."

For members of Jesus' audience not nursing migraines from so much shock and confusion by this time in Jesus' speech, the facetiousness of this statement might have made them laugh.

D: Explain that.

S: Ok.

Jesus' use of "few will find it" can be understood by a simple analogy:

Let's say someone puts out a notice all over the world that anyone who wants to participate in the greatest Eco-Challenge of all time can meet at Mount Everest Base Camp at 1pm on May 4. And there will be a grand prize of ten million dollars to the winner(s).

On that day, let's say 500 people show up.

The guy who organized the event stands up and says, "Thanks for coming, I'm glad so many of you could make it. I'll get right to the point. Here's the challenge..."

Everyone leans forward, on the edge of their seats.

"The challenge is that whoever can walk from here to the summit of Everest *barefooted*, wins!"

Then he grins and adds, "And I'm thinking only a few of you will do it."

I think that's what Jesus meant when he said "few will find it."

The reason for Jesus' facetiousness may have stemmed from the fact that there were some in that society, some in his very audience (the Pharisees and Sadducees), who thought they were accomplishing getting to God by the 'narrow gate of perfection.'

But Jesus will soon give them, and everyone else, the wake-up call of their lives with his Great Reversal: "The first shall be last, and the last shall be first" (Matthew 20:16).

With this statement, Jesus gives another not-so-subtle warning that those who thought they had a lock on 'going to heaven' (the Pharisees and Sadducees), because they thought they were following the Law adequately, were not going to make it that way.

On the other hand, those who thought they had no chance in hell to make it to heaven were going to get to heaven—the tax gatherers and the 'sinners.'

So to sum up—since it's hugely important—contrary to the "narrow gate" traditionally being interpreted as "Jesus is the narrow gate," we see that the narrow gate is actually human moral perfection apart from God. That is why 'few' find it. *(see appendix 2 for a note on the* narrow door *in Luke 13:22-30).*

Still not convinced?

Then ask yourself this: Why would God come to earth from his cushy life in heaven (Philippians 2) to live the life of a servant subjected to a creation that opposed him as an enemy rather than a friend, then that very creation tortures and murders him—a creation he loves and wants to be intimately involved with—if only a few were going to "find it?"

I believe Christ came to earth to make it as easy as possible for people to 'get right with God.'

Why?

Let's take the focus off us humans a moment and look at things from a loving God's perspective.

Christ did this: He came to earth, suffered and died so God could come to us, and live in intimate relationship with us by removing the sin barrier once and for all (Isaiah 43:25).

So did God get what he wanted?

Yes, he did.

Christ put the sin barrier between man and God to death, once and for all. Forever.

When it comes to salvation, 'sin' has never been the issue that keeps people from God, and vice-versa.

God told Abraham, "Go to another land, a land I have picked out for you" (Genesis 12:1-4).

In effect he was asking Abraham, 'Do you agree this is a good and right plan, or not?'

Abraham believed God's plan was good and right, and it was credited to him as righteousness.

Where's the discussion about Abraham's sin?

It's not there.

God simply wanted the DOI to agree with him on this—that humans can never be perfect enough to stand in his presence in their natural selves (1 Corinthians 15:50) and therefore something else was needed (Christ's sacrifice on their behalf).

Could they agree that 'it is *finished*'?

The sin barrier between humanity and God was removed, and all humans are free before God with respect to sin (2 Corinthians 5:19).

D: Whoa! So if there's no longer a sin barrier between humans and God then everyone automatically goes to heaven, right? Is that what you're saying?

S: Well, here's the thing. That's probably not an appropriate way to approach this anymore.

D: Huh?

S: I mean your question. It needs reframing. The theology of 'heaven' and the notion of 'going to heaven after you die' is being rethought and redefined by theologians and thinkers as we speak.

Heaven, or the 'Kingdom of God,' in the Protestant/Evangelical tradition has meant a place, a place where God is now, and then we go *there* to be with God when we die.

That is the traditional view. But heaven, while it *is* God's kingdom, was probably meant by Jesus to be just as much a state of being as a specific geographic location.

We traditionally think of 'eternal life' as being in

heaven with God forever....*after* we die.

But when Jesus spoke of 'eternal life,' he most likely meant a state of *abundant* life, a life that flows with living water.

A good life.

Or more like: *The* Good Life.

The *best* life.

But free-will and evil does still exist. So if we don't want to be with God, or we deliberately want to continue harming the creation he loves and is working to heal and restore (including humans), then from the Bible we can see that in his justice he will deal with it somehow.

We just don't know *exactly* how.

But that's ok.

We can leave it to God and trust that he will deal with it in all fairness, justice and righteousness.

We, however, are free to love.

We are free to follow the example of Jesus and love people no matter how they treat us, whether good or bad.

How we treat someone doesn't need to be contingent on how they treat us.

Not that we should stay in abusive relationships. We see throughout the Bible that even God didn't stay in abusive relationships.

But we have the opportunity to experience the truth that love conquers all.

Forgiveness is better than getting even.

Love is better than holding a grudge.

Doing good to anyone, enemies included, is where life and more life is to be found.

Always.

All the time.

In any situation.

We are free.

We have the key to 'eternal life.'

Life to the most abundant it can possibly be.

The Bible is simply one giant book of God inviting all who are tired of religion (any religion) and the whole 'sin/not sinning' game; all who are done with keeping tabs on how moral or immoral they are and the morality or immorality of those around them; all who are tired of striving for 'sanctification' and growing toward 'Christlikeness'; all who are big-time sinners who don't really care what anyone thinks about them (tax gatherers and prostitutes); all atheists currently devising new moral codes and laws to live by; all who are tired and done with trying to make their lives 'work' in the tyranny of the limited resources of their own finiteness and the limited resources of the physical world we live in—all who are tired of *ALL THAT CRAP*, and simply want to *rest* (Matthew 11:28-30)—are invited to shed those tiresome lifestyles and join the party.

The party starts now.

And this invitation is offered to everyone in the entire world, not just those in the Western hemisphere.

It goes for India, Japan, the Middle East, China, Africa, Southeast Asia—*all* are invited to lay down their striving in useless religion, empty philosophical systems, and 'trying to be good'...and *rest*.

Jesus says in the parable of the Ten Virgins in Matthew 25 that after an incredibly long time had passed, to those who weren't prepared for the party—to those whom Jesus didn't know—the door was *shut* and they were left out of the party.

The religious, the 'righteous,' those who didn't want to lower their pride and jump completely into the boat of 'God did it all so I don't have to,' are left out.

This isn't harsh or unfair.

It's simply *not* forcing people to go where they don't want to go.

No one is 'sent' here, or 'put' there. They simply stay or go where *they choose* to stay or go.

There is no 'us vs. them.' There is no 'in' group and 'out' group. No one is excluded on the basis of their cultural or religious background. No one need be treated harshly or wrongly because they are different from anyone else.

God is inviting the whole human race, all who are weary and down-trodden, all who are tired of rules and rituals (religion) dominating and enslaving their lives. All who are tired of keeping tabs on 'doing right and/or wrong' and living under the shackles of 'trying to be good' (Matthew 11:28-30).

God is inviting all who want freedom, relaxation, and getting as much enjoyment out of life as they possibly can (John 10:10).

All who want to be free of the tyranny of stress and

worry about the limited resources of our own finite, physical selves and let the unlimitable God of the universe take care of everything for us.

God invites us to his party.

Do we want to come?

It's going to be a kick-ass party.

But we don't have to go if we don't want to.

Scene 8

"The Wise Man" Keeps in Context

D: This is really exciting stuff.

S: I think so too. And it's been in the Bible all along. Same words, but very different outcome.

D: It's the same words. There's nothing new. Everything you're talking about—the actual words in the Bible—haven't changed at all.

S: That's the fascinating thing about it.

D: Let's keep going.

S: Throughout the book of Matthew, as far as the DOI are concerned, Jesus spends a great deal of time contrasting two themes: Following the Law to perfection vs. following the Law in hypocrisy.

Jesus has two conclusions on the matter: Following the Law to perfection is the narrow gate that *no one* passes through, and continuing to live in religious hypocrisy after falling the least bit short of perfection puts you squarely on the wide path that leads to destruction.

By default, following the Law in your own power apart from God has to lead to hypocrisy.

But the Pharisees aren't getting it. They're not engaging Jesus with "ears to hear, or eyes to see."

They don't change their attitudes, but continue to confuse the people with their stringent moralizing.

So in Matthew 7:15, Jesus begins a campaign to expose the hypocrisy of the Pharisees in front of the whole nation, by calling them 'false prophets.'[1]

For their whole lives, their whole culture, their whole way of life, the DOI truly believed, "You listen to these folks and give them the highest respect. They speak for God."

And here comes Jesus saying, "No, they don't."

In Matthew 7:21, the masses are hearing for the first time that not all the Pharisees are 'right with God' and therefore all will not necessarily go to heaven.

This is a shocking reversal for the masses to hear. Strangely at this time, Jesus takes the opportunity to also equate himself with God.

I'm sure that wasn't lost on the religious ruling elite either.

Which leads to Matthew 7:24, where Jesus makes this statement: "Anyone who hears these words (how to be perfect) and puts them into practice is like building your life on the rock. If you fail to be morally perfect, it's like building your house on the sand. You will not 'make it' when the 'rain' of God's judgment comes." (*my paraphrase and parenthesis*)

D: Wait a minute! Wait a minute! That's not the way I've ever heard this. In my mind, I'm humming the cutesy Christian children's song, *'The wise man builds his house upon the rock...*"

S: But is that really what we want kids to be singing about?

D: Ha! What do you mean? Is this like our discussion of *This little light of mine...*?

S: Well, yes.

D: Oh, here we go again...

S: I've always heard this passage, and this children's song, interpreted as the wise man builds his life on *Jesus* (the rock), and if not, the rains (hard circumstances of life) come down and shake him up.

This passage of scripture is commonly taught as a wisdom parable about the best way to live your life, as evidenced by the 'wise' man being mentioned.

But maybe there's a better way to interpret this. For two reasons:

First, if I'm supposed to 'build my life on Jesus,' it only motivates me to build a life on 'Jesus' in self-effort (refer to 1 Corinthians 3:7).

And second: *context, context, context.*

Jesus is still talking about following the Law to perfection in our own moral merit apart from God.

D: So if your interpretation is correct, that means we've been teaching our kids through this cute children's song that the wise person (us as believers) will make sure to follow the Mosaic Law to perfection, because if we don't, when the rain of God's final judgment comes tumbling down, we will be destroyed, or 'left out,' i.e. in Hell.

S: Exactly. And is this what we want to teach our children?

D: I guess not. A 'wise man' might want to consider coming up with a new song.

S: Yes. It'd be good for us to leave this passage in context and look at the rest of the New Testament, which bids us to stop striving in 'moral religious lives in order to get to God' and take the loophole of Christ's sacrifice and enter into a life that God builds *for us.*[2]

D: Now that's something I can write a song about.

S: Just don't do it now.

D: Ouch.

S: I'm not saying you're a crappy songwriter, I'm just saying we've got lots more to talk about.

D: Ok, let's keep going.

S: In Matthew 7:28, we see that people approved of what Jesus was saying; he spoke as one who had authority.

D: Possibly they approved because they were being told they could 'out Pharisee the Pharisees.'

S: Good point. Let's imagine for a second how big such a concept is:

For the first time ever, the unwashed masses were hearing that not all Pharisees were 'right' with God.

And for the first time ever, they were being told they themselves had a shot at getting 'right' with God.

Before Jesus came along, this was something reserved only for the 'righteous'—those in the religious ruling elite.

If you weren't in the ruling/teaching elite, you were rabble, a 'sinner' (Luke 18:9-14), a castoff in the tradition of the seemingly 'holier than thou' words of Nehemiah (Nehemiah 13:14;22;29;31).[3]

You were doomed to Hell and destruction, with little or no hope.

The entire DOI had been told their whole lives that their righteousness didn't come close to the righteousness of the Pharisees, which was the righteousness required by God.

Now Jesus was leveling the playing field.

He said, in effect, "You (the unwashed masses) can still get to God, and some (maybe many) of the Pharisees are actually going to Hell."

So the people liked this teaching.

D: Hell yeah, they did!

S: But at this time in DOI history, Jesus wasn't the only one going around claiming to be saying things on behalf of God.

Many were going around claiming to be the Messiah (the next physical king of Israel in the line of David and Solomon), and making grandiose claims about themselves.

So Jesus was doing nothing out of the ordinary in the larger context of society. There were many men who claimed to be the Messiah before, during, and after Jesus' time.[4]

And the Bible says some were doing 'tricks' by the power of demons while claiming authority from God for what they were doing (Matthew 12:24-29).

This meant early on it was important for Jesus to clearly establish by who's—or what—authority he was doing these things.

The masses rightly wondered: "Ok, this Jesus fellow

talks a good game, but why should we believe him? From where does he get the authority to say such things and make such judgments on the ruling class entrusted with God's revelation?"

You see, authority was a very big deal in DOI society.

"By what authority do you do this?" was often asked of Jesus. "By whose authority do you say these things and do these things (miracles)?"

We must also keep in mind that Jesus was a backwater hick, and people were beginning to follow him en masse, something that didn't escape the attention of the religious elite.

So in Matthew chapter 8, Jesus begins to establish his authority.

---

[1] Later, when he fully exposes their hypocrisy and moral bankruptcy and the spiritual and financial oppression of the people, the DOI masses will look back on these words and think, "Oh, ok, we get it now. Don't listen to them—the ruling religious power elite. They do not speak for God. They are false prophets."

[2] Great pictures of what God does for humans are given in Deuteronomy 6, and 2 Samuel 7:1-16.

[3] Not saying that Nehemiah himself intended his words as 'Holier than Thou." Nehemiah was clearly a man obedient to God, a man of God. He meant "Thank God I'm following God even though they aren't" in the context of the Law. He was supposed to follow God even if others weren't. But over time, his words could have been a misconstrued mantra adopted by the Pharisees, so much so that Jesus felt the need to address this 'us and them' attitude in the parable of the Publican and Sinner. So no, it's not Nehemiah's fault. He was a good egg.

[4] Messiah means 'king.' So they were looking for a physical reigning king on earth in the line of Kings David and Solomon.

Scene 9

"Respect My Authori-TIE!"

S: In Matthew chapter 8, Jesus begins to establish his authority as being 'sent' from God. He proves this by a display of power over sickness, disease, and the dark spiritual world (demons). And even the weather.

D: The weather?

S: Yes, even the weather, by calming the storm in Matthew 8:23-27.

D: What's that all about?

S: Consider this: It would've meant a lot to the DOI for Jesus to prove he had the power and authority to change the weather.

They would have known God's statements in the Old Testament about controlling the weather for them in the Promised Land (Deuteronomy 11:13-14).

Taking care of their crops by controlling the weather was part of the original Law contract.

Jesus parallels another Old Testament scripture in order to establish his authority:

> When Jesus saw the crowd around him, he gave orders to cross to the other side of the lake. Then a teacher of the law came to him and said, "Teacher, I will follow you wherever you go." Jesus

> replied, "Foxes have dens and birds have nests, but the Son of Man has no place to lay his head." Another disciple said to him, "Lord, first let me go and bury my father." But Jesus told him, "Follow me, and let the dead bury their own dead."(Matthew 8:18-22)

D: Jesus seems to be unnecessarily harsh to a man who truly wants to follow him. And what's that have to do with Jesus establishing his authority by using the Old Testament?

S: Very good question. Often we interpret this passage to be the importance of putting Christ first in our Christian lives, so we do theological gymnastics and say Jesus didn't literally mean for that man to follow him right that moment, but he was just trying to show the importance of himself as God and our savior, as in "You must have no other Gods before me."

But there might be a better explanation for it.

Besides Abraham and Moses, Elijah was the most respected figure in DOI history (kind of like George Washington and Abraham Lincoln are to Americans).

They are so important, in fact, that we will soon see Elijah and Moses show up with Jesus at the Mount of Transfiguration (Matthew 17:1-8).

So Elijah is a big deal to them.

A really big deal.

He has *authority*.

1 Kings 19:16-21 tells us that at the end of Elijah's ministry, God picked a man named Elisha to be Elijah's successor as a prophet of God. Elijah was to go and find Elisha in a field and symbolically hand over his coat to show him as being an apprentice.

When Elijah finds Elisha, Elisha requests to go home and take care of his parents first before following Elijah.

And Elijah says, "Yes, do that and come on back. Then we'll get started."

Now, in Matthew 8:21-22, Jesus is one-upping this[1] by telling the man before him that he cannot go home and tend to things before following him. He must follow him now.

He's establishing his authority as being *greater* than Elijah.[1]

And this wouldn't have been lost on the DOI.

So Jesus is *not* being a jerk. He's simply establishing his authority in a way the DOI would understand.

And understand they did.

But Jesus ups the authority ante even further in Matthew 9:1 when he equates himself with God by telling a man, "Your sins are forgiven."

The Pharisees knew exactly what Jesus was saying. And to them, it was blasphemy, punishable by death.

D: Jesus is really stirring the pot now, isn't he?

S: Yes. Very much so.

So with all this going on, in Matthew 9 Jesus speaks of the other half of his mission, which is to usher in the kingdom of God.

He begins alluding to the fact that a new way of living with God is coming. And he equates himself with that new way.

In Matthew 9:14-17, Jesus is asked why he doesn't have his followers adhere to the strict fasting codes under the Mosaic Law:

> Then John's disciples came and asked him, "How is it that we and the Pharisees fast often, but your disciples do not fast?" Jesus answered, "How can the guests of the bridegroom mourn while he is with them? The time will come when the bridegroom will be taken from them; then they will fast. No one sews a patch of unshrunk cloth on an old garment, for the patch will pull away from the garment, making the tear worse. Neither do people pour new wine into old wineskins. If they do, the skins will burst; the wine will run out and the wineskins will be ruined. No, they pour new wine into new wineskins, and both are preserved." (Matthew 9:14-17)

In essence, Jesus responds that when the kingdom of God is ushered in, the celebration begins. The work is 'finished.' Nothing else needs to be done. You don't put old wine in new wineskins. The Mosaic Law and the New Covenant under Jesus do not mix. There is no more work of rule-keeping and ritual to be done.

Jesus says the party begins *now*.

We see this theme again when Jesus oddly scolds Martha for working, while her sister Mary enjoys her time hanging out with Jesus in rest (Luke 10:38:42).

Jesus tells Martha that Mary made the right choice.

Now that the Messiah is here, the time for resting and enjoying and living in celebratory community has begun (Acts 4:32-35, 1 Corinthians 11).

In recent Christian history the idea of 'new wineskins' has been co-opted to mean 'new ways of doing ministry,' 'creative ways for believers to *reach* non-believers,' and/or new ways to do 'church' within a new cultural and generational setting.

But this passage is simply announcing that the New Covenant is here. And it will be nothing like the old one. Nothing about the Old Covenant of Law, rules and rituals will fit with the new covenant of rest and life and celebration in freedom.

Now that we're well into Matthew 9, we see another subtle shift in the storyline.

In Matthew 9:35 we're informed that Jesus' healings were evidence that God's kingdom 'was at hand' (to come the moment Christ resurrected).

Just as John the Baptist announced that the coming kingdom was at hand, in the same way, Jesus in Matthew 9 and 10 continues to prepare the people for the coming kingdom.

D: And with Jesus, the coming kingdom was really close.

S: Indeed.

So in Matthew 9:36 and following, Jesus saw that the people were "helpless and harassed, like sheep without a shepherd."

> When he saw the crowds, he had compassion on them, because they were harassed and helpless, like sheep without a shepherd. Then he said to his disciples, "The harvest is plentiful but the workers are few. Ask the Lord of the harvest, therefore, to send out workers into his harvest field." (Matthew 9:36-38)

The people of Israel were being let down by their religious leaders, the Pharisees and Sadducees. With twisted teachings and financial oppression of the masses, these people ran things in a way that only benefited themselves.

At the same time, everyone in the country—the underclasses and the Pharisees alike—were shaken up by Jesus and his demands for perfection under the Law.

Which was exactly his goal.

He *wanted* to shake them up.

All of them.

Being shaken up, they'd be awake and listening.

However, as far as the underclass was concerned, Jesus points out they were floating as "sheep without a shepherd" ready to be "harvested."

The people were primed and ready for kingdom news.

Good kingdom news.

So what to do?

Jesus sends out workers into the harvest.

Now, in the recent Christian era, we have taken these words to be a mantra for the Christian church to evangelize the world.

D: You're saying they're not?

S: I'm saying there might be a better way to look at it.

D: But didn't Jesus say to "Go and make disciples of all nations?" (Matthew 28:19)

S: Yes he did. But in this particular passage he is most likely not teaching that theme.

D: Why do you say that?

S: Because this passage leads to the sending out of the

twelve at the beginning of Matthew 10, which was *not* an evangelizing mission.

Jesus was not sending people out to tell people about Christ and convert them to Christianity.

D: He wasn't?

S: Jesus states the specific point of the mission in the text: "Heal the sick, raise the dead, cleanse those with leprosy, and cast out demons."

That's all they were to do.

Nothing more, nothing less.

> Jesus called his twelve disciples to him and gave them authority to drive out impure spirits and to heal every disease and sickness. These are the names of the twelve apostles: first, Simon (who is called Peter) and his brother Andrew; James son of Zebedee, and his brother John; Philip and Bartholomew; Thomas and Matthew the tax collector; James son of Alphaeus, and Thaddaeus; Simon the Zealot and Judas Iscariot, who betrayed him. These twelve Jesus sent out with the following instructions: 'Do not go among the Gentiles or enter any town of the Samaritans. Go rather to the lost sheep of Israel. As you go, proclaim this message: *The kingdom of heaven has come near.* Heal the sick, raise the dead, cleanse those who have leprosy, drive out demons. Freely you have received; freely give." (Matthew 10:1-8—*italics mine*)

D: You're right, evangelizing and converting aren't in the text. But why wouldn't Jesus want them to evangelize and convert?

S: Because that wasn't what Jesus wanted to accomplish at that time. He clearly stated the goal. To "proclaim the message: The kingdom of heaven has come near."

And think about this: How could they evangelize, or convert people to Christianity, when Jesus hadn't died and rose from the dead yet? The people, including Christ's own disciples, thought Jesus was a political leader or a religious leader who would soon rule the nation in the line of Kings David and Solomon. Nearly no one had an accurate understanding of the true mission of Jesus yet.

D: Good point.

S: So what he was really doing in this 'sending out' mission was establishing his authority.

By healing and casting out demons, Jesus was signaling to the people—in the line of John the Baptist—that the kingdom of God was 'at hand;' that it was 'near.'

John the Baptist baptized people in preparation for the kingdom coming. Now Jesus was saying, the kingdom of God is *really* at hand, it's *very close*, because now the Messiah (that's me) has arrived.[2]

So in light of that, this passage probably should not be used as a model for evangelism, or for how to 'do' missions.

Sending people out 'two by two' is not a necessary model for evangelism and missions. It might be a good, practical way to go about things, but Jesus wasn't mandating a hard and fast rule.

Neither was Jesus advocating the idea of 'looking for the man of peace' (someone 'open' to the gospel— Matthew 10:11) as something for us believers today.

I've heard it been taught that as we try to 'evangelize' people, we should look for someone 'open' to the gospel. And if no one quickly shows interest, Jesus tells us to move on.

But this is not advice for us today.

Not only that, 'moving on' from people who aren't interested doesn't square well with 1 Corinthians 13, which states "love never quits."

D: Are you saying we have to be absolutely 100% committed in love to any given person or friendship we may have for the rest of our lives and into eternity?

S: No, I don't believe so. Because we live in freedom (Galatians 5:1). We can love any friend or random person we meet undyingly until the end of time if we want to, but we're not required to be 100% committed to *any* person, with the exception of our spouses.

By entering into marriage, we are pledging to be 100% committed to love and care for that person for both of our entire lives.

But other than that, in our relationships, we are free. And if we're 'living in the spirit' (Galatians 5:16-18), one thing is certain: Love.

It's automatic.

Not because of our *work*, but by getting ourselves out of the way in rest (Matthew 11:28-30 (NIV), Matthew 5:3 (MSG)) God's spirit of perfect love as presented in 1 Corinthians 13 automatically comes through. This Spirit lives in us and through us (Galatians 2:20). We can block it, we can quench it, but it's there. It doesn't leave.

So when God loves through us, he never quits. As long as we're in friendship or relationship with anyone, in our freedom we can commit to them for as long as we want, or forever. And God will love them through us until forever if that's what we choose.

Ok, after that track, let's pause a moment and look at the timeline of Jesus' mission to usher in the kingdom of God:

First, John the Baptist told people to get ready for Jesus' coming in general.

"Repent,[3] the Kingdom of God is at hand," he said. "It's coming."

His method of getting his point across?

Baptism in water. A foreshadow of fully identifying ourselves—and being fully identified—with Jesus (Baptism means, literally, "to be put into"[4]).

Soon, Jesus would take things a step further and baptize with the Holy Spirit.

And now, in our day, we invite people to God's party (Matthew 25:10).

Our method of getting our point across?

Our free and expansive lives, which includes, but is not limited to, living in and by the Spirit.

We show our faith in the adequacy of what Christ has done by our deed of being free and staying free from all forms of rules, rituals and religion (James 2, Galatians 5:1).

S: Does this make sense?

D: Yes, I think so.

S: I think it sounds *great*.

/thē·*il*·logical/ - 83

¹ God taking things one step further is also evidenced in Jesus' birth. Isaac was born from a mother and father who were physically unable to conceive children because they were too old. Isaac's birth was miraculous, straight from God. And Isaac is the ancestral line of Jesus. However, Jesus birth upped the 'Isaac miracle' a step further by Jesus being miraculously born from a human mother (Mary), but no father. So even if we stretch to think two people in their nineties could possibly have a child, we'd have to say that it was completely impossible for a virgin woman to become pregnant in that day and age. So again, God was clearly pointing out to the DOI, and all humans—including us today—that Jesus was even more special and set-apart than any other person who's ever lived.

² And it's important to note that practically everyone in the DOI, including Peter and most of the disciples, if not all, expected the Messiah to be a physical reigning king, in the line of David and Solomon, who would lead the people in a rebellion to kick out the occupying Romans and re-establish the glory days of Israel. That is what they thought was going to happen, all the way up until, and after, Jesus' death and resurrection. They were only set straight when Jesus taught them after he appeared to them after death. When Jesus asks Peter who do you say I am? And Peter says, 'the Messiah,' Peter was still thinking the physical reigning king. How do we know this? Because Peter was prepared to start the rebellion by slicing off a man's ear who tried to take Jesus into custody. Maybe he intended to hack the guy in the head, but missed, possibly because it was in the middle of the night and he was exhausted.

³ 'Repent,' an oft used and abused word, simply means to 'change your mind about things.' To think about what it means that God is on his way. Consider the path your life is currently headed down, and make changes if necessary.

⁴ And this is exactly what Paul means in Galatians 2:20, and in every verse where he mentions being 'in Christ.' We are identified fully with Christ, and it is no longer I (we) who live, but Christ lives in me (us). Paul is fully identified with Christ. There is no process of sanctification, no cycles of repentance and continually coming back to the foot of the cross. No. He is fully identified right now. Paul no longer

lives, but Christ lives in him. He is filled with the Spirit, 'living by the Spirit' as opposed to living according to the flesh...etc, etc. It's a matter of identification, not a matter of striving in moral effort, or a process of slowly becoming more Christ-like over time. Christ lives in and through us right now. It is no longer us who live, but Christ lives in us.

Scene 10

Burdened Under the Lightness of Being

D: One thing's for sure, I've had way too much coffee. But I really like this discussion and don't want to stop.

S: Then let's keep going. I think we're in Matthew 10. Ah, yes. Coming upon the famous 'video screen' passage of Matthew 10:26: "So do not be afraid of them, for there is nothing concealed that will not be disclosed, or hidden that will not be made known."

D: Oh, man, I remember sitting in church as a kid hearing the pastor refer to this verse and say, "When we one day die and stand before God, a giant movie screen will come down and our whole lives will be played for all to see, and we'll be answerable to God for all we've done."

S: Wow. What a weight to throw on people!

D: Since then, sadly I've run into quite a few people who've heard this passage taught this way.

S: But we must ask ourselves: Is that really what Jesus meant when he said, "There is nothing concealed that will not be disclosed, or hidden that will not be made known?"

Jesus encouraged those in the DOI who would be persecuted for his sake by saying, "One day, it will be known to everyone that I am who I say I am, and that everything I've told you is true. So be encouraged when you face hard times from people who are against you. When all is said and done, you'll be shown to be on the winning side." (*my paraphrase*)

This is clear because he tells them immediately afterward that they are not to be afraid of those who can only kill the body but cannot kill the soul (Matthew 10:28).

Jesus is urging them to pick teams now. Decide to be on *my* team though people will give you a hard time and it will seem unpopular. Because in the end it's going to be evident to all that Jesus is the winning team. So buy your jersey and hop on the band-wagon.

With all this in mind, let's go on to Matthew 10:32-33: "Whoever acknowledges me before men, I will also acknowledge him before my Father in heaven. But whoever disowns me before men, I will disown him before my Father in heaven."

Some have understood these verses to be in regard to 'backsliding' Christians, but Jesus is simply speaking of a rejection in people's hearts of Jesus and God's plan.

One reason we know this is a more accurate interpretation is because Peter denied Christ by disowning him in public *three times*.

And was he rejected by God?

No.

Ok, let's move on:

The odd, seemingly violent statements of Jesus in Matthew 10:34-37 are simply saying this is the most important thing ever in life. Give this the top priority. It cannot be secondary. It cannot, and should not, be taken lightly.

> "Do not suppose that I have come to bring peace to the earth. I did not come to bring peace, but a sword. For I have come to turn
>
>> 'a man against his father, a daughter against her mother, a daughter-in-law against her mother-in-law—a man's enemies will be the members of his own household.'
>
> "Anyone who loves their father or mother more than me is not worthy of me; anyone who loves their son or daughter more than me is not worthy of me." (Matthew 10:34-37)

Again, we can look back to the Elijah/Elisha allusion with Elisha wanting to go back to tend to his family first.

Spiritually, we know that the coming of the kingdom of God was a huge battle between God and Satan. The kingdom was not ushered in with the quietness of a lamb, but through a war in the spiritual realm unlike any spiritual battle before it (Revelation 12).

Jesus' odd, seemingly caustic charge to Peter to "Get behind me Satan!" (Matthew 16:23) shows that the physical world and spiritual world are intimately intertwined, and sometimes God pulls back the curtain to give us a glimpse of it. That's what the entire book of Revelation is about. A revelation—a *revealing*—of the spiritual world.

Let's go on to Matthew 11:

At the beginning of this chapter, John the Baptist is in prison and seems to be struggling with doubt. Hard to blame him since he's in prison even though the Messiah, who John probably thought was the best person to help him out of his crappy circumstance, is running around the countryside and doing nothing at all to rescue him.

So John sends his disciples to question Jesus: "Are you the Messiah? Or should we look for someone else?"

Jesus' reply is this:

> "Go back and report to John what you hear and see: The blind receive sight, the lame walk, those who have leprosy are cleansed, the deaf hear, the dead are raised, and the good news is proclaimed to the poor. Blessed is anyone who does not stumble on account of me." (Matthew 11:4-6)

Jesus tells John's disciples, "My authority has been established. The miracles I've performed are evidence—and the good news is being preached to the poor."

These abilities not only proved his authority, they were evidence that he was the one promised to come. He's reassuring John that while he may be languishing in prison, he can have faith that Jesus is fulfilling the predictions of the prophet Isaiah (Isaiah 35:5-6 and 61:1).

Ok, here comes a really exciting bit. A major shift in the story. The turning point of the whole book of Matthew.

Jesus' authority has been established, and the ruling elites are by and large rejecting it, though not all of them. Some were actually beginning to follow Jesus.

However, tensions were running extremely high as everyone was feeling the full weight of Jesus' shackling teachings under the Law. Everyone.

So with all eyes on him, Jesus is about to turn everything on its head and change the way all of humanity has ever lived in relation to God.

He drops this huge bombshell in Matthew 11:25-30: "My burden is easy, my yoke is light..."

What?

Isn't this the same guy who told everyone they had to "be perfect?"

Isn't this the guy who was going to lead everyone on a mission to "out Pharisee the Pharisees?" To chop off body parts if they caused them to sin, and they'll end up in Hell if they don't?

What gives?

This is what gives:

After shackling the people with the impossibility of what it means to live perfectly under the Law, in a genius reversal, Jesus says, "Come to me, all who are weary and burdened, and I will give you rest. Take my yoke upon you and learn from me, for I am gentle and humble in heart, and you will find rest for your souls. For my yoke is easy and my burden is light" (Matthew 11:28-30).

The masses must have thought: "Is this guy crazy? Exactly how is your burden 'light'? You've been laying a heavy load on us since you first opened your mouth! What are you talking about?"

But think about this: They've seen Jesus perform physical healings for free. Now he's setting them up to understand salvation is for free, and not by good works or moral merit under the Law apart from God.

All they have to do is identify themselves with him. They could rest in their identity in him. He made their burden light. He carried the load for them. And today, he carries the load for us as well. All of it.

He fulfilled the Law so we don't have to.[1]

Can you imagine the relief and joy from the common folk when they finally understood this after Jesus' death and resurrection?

Because at this time, still almost no one really knew what was going on with this guy. But this 'rest' was foreshadowed in one of the 'Ten Commandments' laws of the Old Testament as explained in Hebrews 4—The Sabbath day. This was a physical day of rest built into the DOI work week to foreshadow the rest we have for all time in that Jesus did the work of salvation for us. It is finished. (God also had the concept of rest threaded through other parts of the Old Testament—See Exodus 33:14.)

S: So does this make sense?

D: I think it does. Give me more.

S: Ok.

Moving into Matthew 13, Jesus is going to present a few parables that describe the coming kingdom of God; what this kingdom looks like.

He starts by giving an enigmatic statement:

> He (Jesus) said to them, "Therefore every teacher of the law who has become a disciple in the kingdom of heaven is like the owner of a house who brings out of his storeroom new treasures as well as old." (Matthew 13:52)

These teachers of the Law had been entrusted with the old way (the Mosaic Law), but now, Jesus said, some of them would be pointing to and following the 'new way'—the legal loophole of Christ's sacrifice.

With this statement, Jesus was saying that the much

maligned Pharisees were invited to the same lightness of being offered the common masses. They were invited to immediately unshackle themselves from the Law and be free.

To Jesus, being a Pharisee wasn't the problem. The issue was the same as for everyone else: Stay with shackling religion, or run to freedom.

Jesus was announcing freedom; hoping they'd have ears to hear it, eyes to see it. And some of them would. And did (John 3:1-21).

Because it was great news.

The greatest news ever given in the history of humanity.

S: You getting hungry yet?

D: Sort of. But I want to keep going.

S: Well, I hope you like seafood, because this next section has lots of it.

D: What do you mean?

---

[1] No one except the DOI were ever under the Law. No one else has ever been required to fulfill the Law (Romans 1 and 2). Salvation for everyone (including the DOI) has never been about the works of the Law or the Mosaic Law. The Bible is clear that salvation has always been a matter of faith and trust in God's plan(s), and never in the actual works or Law, because God knew from the beginning of time that no one, not even the DOI, could live perfect lives. The Old Testament clearly shows this. Everything in the Mosaic Law pointed to this fact, pointed to the need for a 'scapegoat'; another way to accomplish the perfection God requires. Everything pointed to the coming of Jesus. Another good question is this: Why did God have people from surrounding nations

convert to Judaism if salvation wasn't found in becoming a grafted member of the DOI? Well, conversion wasn't for 'salvation' but it grafted you into the Mosaic Law contract as a physical member of the DOI (this is what the mandated ritual of circumcision was for). Now, as a member of the DOI, if you upheld the Law and its rituals, the blessings of God promised to the DOI applied to you as well. And the promised blessings were nothing short of living life in the Garden of Eden. And that was a pretty good deal. After the death and resurrection of Christ, God made the Garden of Eden available to everyone.

Scene 11

Every Time I Sea Food, I Eat It!

S: We all know this next story.

The famous feeding of the 5,000, and the lesser known feeding of the 4,000, which never got as good of billing.

D: Poor feeding of the 4,000. But I love seafood. Let's go with this. And I think I'll go up and get some fish tacos after we talk about this. You want one?

S: Sure. But for now, I've generally heard this story taught that Jesus' miraculous feeding of the 5,000, and the 4,000, was about we believers giving our meager talents, skills and gifting to God so he can multiply them in ministry and service to others.

But I'm not sure that's it.

I think Jesus' intention with these two miraculous feedings (Matthew 14:13-21, Matthew 15:29-39) was to show that everything depends on Jesus, and nothing depends on us.

This miracle is recounted in John 6, where we hear the utter exasperation in Philip's voice.

In verse 7, after Jesus asked the disciples to feed the huge crowd, Philip looks over the situation and exclaims, "It would take more than half a year's wages to buy enough bread for each one to have a bite!"

He was utterly overwhelmed by the impossibility of it.

The *impossibility*.

So everything about God's work depends on God's power, not our power. Not our self-effort, not our 'work' for God.

D: To be clear, you're saying the feeding of the 5,000 and 4,000 is not 'if you give a little of your efforts and talents to God, he will multiply it miraculously for the kingdom work?' Are you sure that's not correct?

S: Yes, because 'giving our little bit to God so he can multiply it' is self-effort. That would be what *we* do for God, then he 'blesses' it. In other words, 'God helps those who help themselves,' which is contrary to anything we find in the New Testament.

D: So it looks like our role is to surrender. When Philip saw it was impossible, he needed to surrender what he could see in the natural world to the power of God.

S: And by doing that, he saw the power of God. He saw God.

Ok, go get your tacos, then let's go on to Matthew 15, where again, Jesus exposes the hypocrisy of the Pharisees and Sadducees. I'll wait.

(Time passes)

D: I'm back.

S: In Matthew 15:10-20, the inside/outside of the cup analogy is revisited:

> Jesus called the crowd to him and said, "Listen and understand. What goes into someone's mouth does not defile them, but what comes out of their mouth, that is what defiles them."

Then the disciples came to him and asked, "Do you know that the Pharisees were offended when they heard this?' He replied, "Every plant that my heavenly Father has not planted will be pulled up by the roots. Leave them; they are blind guides. If the blind lead the blind, both will fall into a pit."

Peter said, "Explain the parable to us."

"Are you still so dull?" Jesus asked them. "Don't you see that whatever enters the mouth goes into the stomach and then out of the body? But the things that come out of a person's mouth come from the heart, and these defile them. For out of the heart come evil thoughts— murder, adultery, sexual immorality, theft, false testimony, slander. These are what defile a person; but eating with unwashed hands does not defile them." (Matthew 15:10-20)

Again, Jesus tells them, the issue between humans and God is not an issue of outward behavior or moral good works.

The issue is that the heart is wicked (Jeremiah 17:9). Human nature is by its nature opposed and contrary to God. So a more drastic and dramatic solution is needed than merely following some of the Law, picking and choosing to do some good works, or some rituals, as defined and interpreted by human religiosity.

What is needed is a replacement of our very nature in our inner-most beings.

In Matthew 16:21, Jesus begins to tell the disciples he's going to be handed over to the authorities to be executed and on the third day he will rise from the dead.

And they all said, *Huh*?

They just didn't get it.

Jesus tells them in Matthew 16:24-27 the key to life is to be identified with his death and resurrection. That is how you will find life and freedom, as opposed to slavery to sin and death.

This follows on the heels of his statement that his burden is light and his yoke is easy:

> Then Jesus said to his disciples, "Whoever wants to be my disciple must deny themselves and take up their cross and follow me. For whoever wants to save their life will lose it, but whoever loses their life for me will find it. What good will it be for someone to gain the whole world, yet forfeit their soul? Or what can anyone give in exchange for their soul? For the Son of Man is going to come in his Father's glory with his angels, and then he will reward each person according to what they have done." (Matthew 16:24-27)

D: But that last part says, "For whoever wants to save their life will lose it, but whoever loses their life for me will find it." What about that?

S: We must be identified with Christ's death and resurrection (Galatians 2:20). And this is a one-time thing. A one-time decision, possibly in a split-second, as we agree in our hearts that Jesus' finished work on the cross is good and sufficient for us to be reconciled to God (2 Corinthians 5:20).

Galatians 2:20 is clear. Paul lost his life to God *once*, in a *one-time* decision: "I have been crucified with Christ. It is no longer I who live, but Christ lives in me." Now he is eternally identified with Christ.

It's not a continual decision to be made day by day. It happened once.

D: But Jesus says 'Pick up your cross *daily*."

S: Yes. Once we are identified fully with Christ,

Galatians 2:20 is true of us every day.

It's not living in our effort, but living identified with Christ's sacrifice on the cross as the Spirit of God lives in and through us. Our sin nature was put to death once and for all on the cross.

We lose our life once to God, and needn't do it again.

S: Does that make sense?

D: I think it does.

S: Jesus urges the DOI to lose their old sinful selves and be identified with him.

He asks them to take a risk.

A huge risk, as it turns out, since he's asking them to make a decision that goes against everything they've ever been taught. He urges them to become "ignorant like children" and go against the grain of their culture.

And in Matthew 16:27, he does something great. Something God always does when he asks us to take a huge risk and trust him in faith—he throws them a bone.

D: A what?

S: Like throwing a dog a bone. God does something good for us to show he's there; that he's with us. He does something supernatural, or natural, to show us we can trust him.

He throws us a bone.

Throughout the Bible, even in the New Testament, we see God confirming himself to those who seek him.

God isn't looking for us to have 'blind faith.' There's

nothing blind about following God. If you want to see God, just ask. He wants to show himself to people.

D: Are you crazy?

S: No, I've seen it happen. It's amazing when God shows up.

D: I'll take your word for it for now, but I'm still skeptical. I have to admit I've never 'seen' God, and I'm nearing 40 years-old.

S: It's all up to God and his timing. That's part of trust.

In Matthew 16:27 Jesus informs the disciples that a few of them are about to see him as God in a tangible way.

Then we have an unfortunate chapter break between Matthew 16 and 17.

In Matthew 16:28, Jesus tells them, "Some who are standing here will not taste death before they see the Son of Man coming in his kingdom."

Which leads straight to 17:1, where six days later, Peter, James and John go up a hill in Galilee and see Jesus in his 'kingdom glory.'

This is commonly called The Transfiguration:

> After six days Jesus took with him Peter, James and John the brother of James, and led them up a high mountain by themselves. There he was transfigured before them. His face shone like the sun, and his clothes became as white as the light. Just then there appeared before them Moses and Elijah, talking with Jesus.
>
> Peter said to Jesus, "Lord, it is good for us to be

here. If you wish, I will put up three shelters—one for you, one for Moses and one for Elijah."

While he was still speaking, a bright cloud covered them, and a voice from the cloud said, "This is my Son, whom I love; with him I am well pleased. Listen to him!"

When the disciples heard this, they fell facedown to the ground, terrified. But Jesus came and touched them. "Get up," he said. "Don't be afraid." When they looked up, they saw no one except Jesus.

As they were coming down the mountain, Jesus instructed them, "Don't tell anyone what you have seen, until the Son of Man has been raised from the dead." (Matthew 17:1-9)

D: I've always heard this event means we'll experience euphoric 'mountaintop' times, like a spiritual high, on occasion in our Christian lives. Times that are emotionally fun and spiritually rewarding. And these times will be so good, that like Peter, we'll want to 'pitch a tent' right there and stay in that state of spiritual euphoria forever.

But, sadly, eventually we have to come down from the mountain. Then it's back to the grindstone. Back to the hard work of serving the masses again, with all their glaring unmet needs. Back to "bearing our cross" as we "lose our lives so that we may gain them."

S: But I'm not so sure that's what the passage was supposed to mean for us.

D: How do you know?

S: Well, first, because of what we said earlier about 'bearing our cross' and 'losing our lives.'

And second, because of Galatians chapter 3 and

Ephesians 2:8-9, which states, 'For it is by grace you have been saved, though faith—and this not from yourselves, it is the gift of God—not by works, so that no one can boast.'

We did nothing in our effort to gain 'salvation,' so Paul says we are to do nothing in our own efforts to live our daily lives as Christians.

D: So we do nothing at all? Is that what you're saying?

S: Well...yes. We are to put forth no hoping and striving (effort) as we try to manipulate outcomes in our own strength and power.

Instead we rest in our spirits and get ourselves out of the way so God can do everything (Matthew 5:3, Galatians 3, I John).

Where in these verses I've mentioned is any of my effort needed?

In light of all this, I doubt Jesus expected the disciples to come off the mountain and 'get back to the grindstone of serving people.'

The disciples didn't 'grind out' serving the masses. They were to get themselves out of the way and let Jesus do it with God's direction and power (feeding of thousands, trips involving healing and casting-out demons, etc.)

After Jesus' death and resurrection, we believers come off the mountain and continue to live exactly as we did *on* the mountain.

In rest, being led to serve and help others in the power of God's spirit; in God's power and plan, not ours.

We are weak. God is strong.

We are jars of clay. God is the infinite power of the universe.

There are no peaks and valleys on the proverbial 'roller-coaster ride' of the Christian life.

D: Ok, you've convinced me. I want to live in rest and follow the leading and power of the Spirit. But what does that mean? What does it look like?

S: Paul would say it means live in and by the Spirit (Galatians 5:16-18).

D: Yes, but what do we do?

S: Live your everyday life by the Spirit in rest.

D: Yes, but what do we do?

S: Live by the Spirit in rest.

D: What do we do? What does it look like?

S: Live by the Spirit. In rest.

D: But how does that accomplish anything?

S: Live in rest in your inner-spirit and in the power and leading of God's spirit.

D: But how will we get anything done?

S: By resting in our spirits as we live in the power and leading of the Spirit.

D: I know. But how will I know if I'm accomplishing anything? How can I measure what myself and others are doing? How do I tell if myself and others are progressing?

S: By living in the power and leading of the Spirit.

D: Arrrgggh! But what does that mean? What does that tangibly look like? What do we do? How do I know if others around me are doing this too?

S: Feeling the need to judge yourself? Others? Wanting to make God manageable? This is what it looks like: Whatever the living, active spirit of God wants it to look like.

D: Oh...now I get it.

Scene 12

Excommunicated From My Church For Not Upholding the Law of Moses

---

S: Now that we got all that settled...

D: I'm still a little fuzzy on all this.

S: It's fun to talk about, though, isn't it?

D: Yes, I'm enjoying the conversation. Good stuff to think about.

S: Well grab another cup of coffee and a taco and let's keep rolling:

At the beginning of Matthew 18, Jesus makes another shocking statement when he says forget about what you know. What God is looking for is simple trust. It's not complicated or complex. The one who trusts the most fully, the most naively, is the greatest in the kingdom of God.

> At that time the disciples came to Jesus and asked, "Who, then, is the greatest in the kingdom of heaven?" He called a little child to him, and placed the child among them. And he said: "Truly I tell you, unless you change and become like little children, you will never enter the kingdom of heaven. Therefore, whoever takes the lowly position of this child is the greatest in the kingdom of heaven. And

> whoever welcomes one such child in my name welcomes me.
>
> "If anyone causes one of these little ones—those who believe in me—to stumble, it would be better for them to have a large millstone hung around their neck and to be drowned in the depths of the sea. Woe to the world because of the things that cause people to stumble! Such things must come, but woe to the person through whom they come! If your hand or your foot causes you to stumble, cut it off and throw it away. It is better for you to enter life maimed or crippled than to have two hands or two feet and be thrown into eternal fire. And if your eye causes you to stumble, gouge it out and throw it away. It is better for you to enter life with one eye than to have two eyes and be thrown into the fire of hell.
>
> "See that you do not despise one of these little ones. For I tell you that their angels in heaven always see the face of my Father in heaven." (Mathew 18:1-10)

Jesus is taking another dig at the Pharisees. They think they 'know,' but they don't. So Jesus tells everyone, be like someone who doesn't 'know.' Be naïve like a child. Don't be like the Pharisees who think they are mature and 'know.'

D: I always thought it was cool that Jesus loved children and carried around sheep.

S: Well, he does love children, but I'm not so sure about the sheep carrying thing. What I do know is that next he's repeating the thing about eye gouging that he first mentioned back in Matthew 5, this time addressing it directly to the Pharisees to make sure everyone is aware once and for all that getting to God by self-effort is totally impossible.

D: You're right, this is the second time he's talking

about eye gouging and foot chopping.

S: Yes, and that's how we know for sure we're still in context with Jesus not talking to believers, but teaching those under the Law how to be perfect under the Law.

D: So the Sermon on the Mount isn't just Matthew 5-7? Jesus is still teaching Law to those under the Law here in Matthew 18?

S: That's right.

D: Wow.

S: It's true.

At the beginning of Matthew 18, the disciples ask Jesus who will be greatest in the kingdom with the anticipation of hearing the obvious answer: *the Pharisees*. Of course he's going to say the Pharisees, right? The Pharisees were the most righteous, the closest to God, the 'Popes' of their generation.

But Jesus says they're far from the most righteous and far from being closest to God.

And in his following statements, Jesus indicts them for leading people into religious hypocrisy and teaching the people falsely about God.

Jesus again points out their religious hypocrisy, then follows it up with a story about a lost sheep.

D: I know this one. It's about 'backslidden' Christians, right? People who began living as Christians then 'fell away?' Like the prodigal son parable, right?

S: Well, that's what's been taught, but I'm not sure it's what Jesus meant.

> "What do you think? If a man owns a hundred sheep, and one of them wanders away, will he not leave the ninety-nine on the hills and go to look for the one that wandered off? And if he finds it, truly I tell you, he is happier about that one sheep than about the ninety-nine that did not wander off. In the same way your Father in heaven is not willing that any of these little ones should perish." (Matthew 18:12-14)

Remember that one of the DOI's biggest problems was they thought they were 'the chosen people of God' and everyone else, the Gentiles, were excluded from God and God's blessings.

And they were perfectly happy believing that.

But contrary to God only blessing the DOI, Jesus tells them God will actually leave the 99[1] to rescue, or bring into his fold, the one that is lost. The 'one' being everyone outside the DOI.

Jesus also meant, with the Pharisees standing right in front of him, the 'one' as the DOI masses outside the religious ruling elite. And this was insulting enough for the Pharisees to want to kill him.

Be it the DOI unwashed masses or Gentile 'dogs,' God never wants any humans choked off from access to himself, nor does he ever want to limit his own full access to *them*.

And to the person who chokes others off from access to God, Jesus says it's better for them to have a millstone tied around their neck and drown in the sea than to be found on the wrong side of God on this issue (Mark 9:42).

That's how serious God takes the matter.

He is very serious, as he should be.

God's love and life are the one place we find true freedom. It's our one and ultimate escape from the tyranny of human limitation and the limitation of our physical existence.

For this reason, Jesus doesn't tolerate false teaching about God. God is very protective about his reputation.[2]

False teaching chokes people off from access to God. It chokes them off from freedom. It chokes them off from finding life.

Conversely, it prevents God from access to people who've turned away in intellectual hopelessness in light of the obvious sham of religious hypocrisy and exploitation.

Jesus taught that the kingdom of heaven and religious hypocrisy both equally spread like wildfire—a little goes a long way. But one is for good, the other for destruction (Matthew 13:33; Mathew 16:6,11,12).

D: Wow. This whole passage is genius.

S: I agree. And that brings us to Matthew 18:15-17:

> "If your brother or sister sins, go and point out their fault, just between the two of you. If they listen to you, you have won them over. But if they will not listen, take one or two others along, so that 'every matter may be established by the testimony of two or three witnesses.' If they still refuse to listen, tell it to the church; and if they refuse to listen even to the church, treat them as you would a pagan or a tax collector." (Matthew 18:15-17)

D: Yes, the church discipline verses.

S: Well...

D: You're not seriously going to say this isn't about

church discipline, are you?

S: Well, ask yourself this question: Would Jesus really be addressing 'church' discipline when the church hasn't yet been established? The 'church' wasn't established until Acts 2.

D: But what about the disciples? Weren't they the first church?

S: Actually...no. Not before Jesus' death anyway. When Jesus was alive as a man, the disciples were not believers as we think of Christians today. They were followers of a Rabbi, thinking this rabbi was, or might be, the Messiah, which to them meant a political king who would liberate Israel from Rome in the line of Kings David and Solomon.

D: Is it possible Jesus was referring to the future?

S: That might be the case, but there's no indication in the text he's talking about the future. When Jesus addresses future events, or addresses future believers, the text always indicates this.

D: So what is Matthew 18:15-17 about?

S: Jesus is still teaching in the context of Law. These verses are sandwiched between the teaching of the Wandering Sheep and the Parable of the Unmerciful Servant. Both are addressed, and pertain to, those under the Law.

So would it make sense to pull these three verses out of that context and say they're addressed to us?

D: I can see your point.

S: Contrary to this being about church discipline in our day, Jesus is teaching a method for dealing with someone who 'sins against you' or 'hurts you' under the Law (Deuteronomy 19:15).

This passage is a lead-in to a discussion between Peter and Jesus in the next chapter where Jesus expounds on his teaching of sin and debt and harming others (and God) and forgiveness—and it's all under the *Law*.

D: If what you're saying is accurate, why did translators use the word 'church' in Matthew 18:17?

S: The word translated 'church' is *'ekklesia,'* which in the Greek simply means a group, or a crowd, an assembly, a multitude, or a meeting of a city's population. Translators of the Bible translated it 'church' possibly under the assumption that Jesus' teachings were always meant for Christians, not meant to teach Law to those under the Law (the DOI). So if Jesus is referring to 'brothers' (better translated 'fellow disciples'), then people may have assumed he's talking about the 'church,' an assembly of 'believers,' or 'fellow disciples.'

But we know from the context and Deuteronomy 19:15 that Jesus was teaching Law to those under the Law, so when he said *'ekklesia,'* what he probably meant was 'a gathering of people,' or 'a multitude of people.'

So if someone sins against you under the Law, deal with it privately, and if the person doesn't respond, take it before the multitudes.

Under Moses, the tribes wandering in the wilderness set up a system of courts to air grievances. When they arrived in the Promised Land, they had similar instructions for how to deal with wrongs (sins) committed against one another (Deuteronomy 19:15).

A large part of Jesus' mission on earth was to expound on the Law as he perfectly lived it out. He taught the masses the Law as God meant it to be lived out. The ruling Pharisees and Sadducees had bastardized pretty much all of God's Law to make it manageable to themselves.

But Jesus cut through all that and taught the Law exactly as God meant it to be. Again, this makes a lot of sense if we look at the four gospel books as the last four books of the Old Testament.

Jesus was careful to say, "I didn't come to abolish the law, but to fulfill it." And by fulfilling it on our behalf, he nullified its demanding edicts. The Law does not pass away, but it's been fulfilled by God on our behalf. So we are no longer 'under the Law.' Any of it. Any of us.

D: That's good stuff. But let me get this straight: So Matthew 18:15-17 is not about dealing with those who sin against us in the church today. It's not about 'church' discipline.[3] Is that what you're saying?

S: Correct. I think the context is clear on that.

D: So are you saying that nothing Jesus said is a universal principal that applies to us today?

S: No, I wouldn't say that's true at all. The words of Jesus are very valuable to us today. The book of John was written with the intent of emphasizing Jesus' divinity. And Jesus directly addresses those who would be believers after his death at several important times in John's gospel. Also, sometimes the writers of the New Testament reiterate principles Jesus taught, showing that they are for us today. And *that* is when Jesus' words apply to us.

Paul does this on several occasions. But we must be careful: We can never teach Matthew 18:12-17 as being for us. It has to stay in the context of its audience. When we are teaching or interpreting what pertains to us today, we can only do this with Jesus' words or statements if the New Testament writers from Acts to Revelation tell us we can. Otherwise, most of Jesus' words were for the DOI, and for those who haven't yet embraced Christ today, and to those people only.

As believers, we're mostly a 'fly on the wall' peering into the life and words of Jesus.

We need to understand that the four gospels were really just lengthy 'evangelistic' tracts. The target audience for Matthew, Mark, Luke, and John were those who didn't yet believe in Christ, those who didn't yet understand who Jesus was, or what the whole 'Jesus thing' was about.

These men did not write these books with the intention of spreading the sayings of someone who wanted to start a new religion. That was never the intention of the four books of the gospels.[4]

To conclude, thankfully this passage in Matthew 18 does not seem to be about church discipline and our traditional notions of what sin is–smoking, drinking, immoral sex, gossip, that kind of stuff.

D: I'm really starting to see how these ideas, when taken to logical conclusions, give us a clearer perspective on Jesus' mission and his words.

S: And it also clears up a lot of contradictions that have plagued the hearts and minds of theologians for centuries.

---

[1] The 99 being the DOI.

[2] So everyone can look at God in a fair and just way, and make their decision if they want to be reconciled to him as

their friend (2 Corinthians 5:20), or not.

[3] The New Testament from Acts to Revelation gives plenty of good advice for having and maintaining a 'healthy' community of believers. Matthew 18 should *not* be used or referred to as any kind of a model for 'church' life. This was not Jesus' intent in this passage.

[4] The four gospels were written by authors with a specific emphasis, or theme, in mind. No one gospel book can stand alone. They are all intertwined ingeniously (by God's design) to give a complete picture of Christ, who he was, and what he came to do. Matthew emphasizes Jesus' mission to fulfill the Law and usher in the kingdom of God. Mark emphasizes Jesus' authority by focusing mostly on the miracles of Jesus. Luke writes his book in journalistic reporting style, emphasizing Jesus' downplaying of what he did. Luke often relates Jesus telling people 'tell no one what you've seen and/or experienced.' In this, Luke was communicating to his friend Theophilus (the person Luke's 'letter' was addressed to) that Jesus was not like all the other men going around claiming to be 'The Messiah.' Luke shows his friend that Jesus was *not* trying to start a new 'religion,' or trying to draw attention to himself to create fame or start a movement. Luke accomplishes telling his friend that Jesus was *entirely different* in what he claimed and how he went about things. John emphasizes the divinity of Jesus, that Jesus clearly equated himself with God.

Scene 13

Christians in God's Torture Chamber?

S: To introduce our next topic, let me tell you a story. Then we're going to discuss two things: a parable and a person.

D: My coffee's still steaming. I'm ready to go.

S: Recently I was sitting in a small group bible study with several married couples with small children and a few single adults.

The leader of the group began the meeting by showing a video. A church acted out Matthew 18:21-35, the Parable of the Unmerciful Servant, in a modern setting:

> Then Peter came to Jesus and asked, "Lord, how many times shall I forgive my brother or sister who sins against me? Up to seven times?"
>
> Jesus answered, "I tell you, not seven times, but seventy-seven times.
>
> "Therefore, the kingdom of heaven is like a king who wanted to settle accounts with his servants. As he began the settlement, a man who owed him ten thousand bags of gold was brought to him. Since he was not able to pay, the master ordered that he and his wife and his children and all that he had be sold to repay the debt.

"At this the servant fell on his knees before him. 'Be patient with me,' he begged, 'and I will pay back everything.' The servant's master took pity on him, canceled the debt and let him go.

"But when that servant went out, he found one of his fellow servants who owed him a hundred silver coins. He grabbed him and began to choke him. 'Pay back what you owe me!' he demanded.

"His fellow servant fell to his knees and begged him, 'Be patient with me, and I will pay it back.'

"But he refused. Instead, he went off and had the man thrown into prison until he could pay the debt. When the other servants saw what had happened, they were outraged and went and told their master everything that had happened.

"Then the master called the servant in. 'You wicked servant,' he said, 'I canceled all that debt of yours because you begged me to. Shouldn't you have had mercy on your fellow servant just as I had on you?' In anger his master handed him over to the jailers to be tortured, until he should pay back all he owed.

"This is how my heavenly Father will treat each of you unless you forgive your brother from your heart." (Matthew 18:21-35)

In the video, a credit card company forgave a man thousands of dollars of debt. Then he turned around and throttled his next-door-neighbor who owed him five dollars.

At the end of the video, a voice-over read the exact words of Matthew 18:21-35.

And everything was fine in my head until the last sentence: "In anger, his master turned him over to the jailors to be *tortured*, until he should pay back all he owed. This is how my heavenly father will *treat each of you* unless you forgive your brother from your heart." (*italics mine*)

What shocked me most was that everyone in the room was so used to hearing this parable, the inflammatory language at the end just rolled over glazed faces without notice.

To me, that sentence of torture was like the blast of a siren.

I looked at the children in front of me, and thought, *Is this really what Jesus was saying to us as believers? That if we don't forgive everyone all the time, we'll end up in God's torture chamber?*

I don't think it's what Jesus had in mind.

Clearly that sentence sounds more like *condemnation* than love, grace and forgiveness. But if we are to take it at face value as being addressed to *us as believers today*, then it's massively inconsistent with the rest of the New Testament.

Not long after this incident, I read a book where the author cited this parable, then ended his commentary by saying, "This is a challenge to us."

But again, is this a challenge to *us*?

At the beginning of the parable, Peter asked Jesus, "How many times should I forgive—seven times?"

Peter asked this because everyone in that day was working overtime figuring out how to make the Law manageable.

But Jesus doesn't take the bait. Instead he says, "No, you are to forgive seventy times seven," which was hyperbole for every single time someone sins against you.

So why would Jesus tell Peter to do this (and by extrapolation, we should do this) if Paul is going to turn around and say living the Christian life isn't about focusing on the Law, but living by the Spirit?

The two are contradictory ideas.

It's illogical.

D: Hmm. That really is food for thought.

S: Let's switch over to Matthew 19 for a moment where a pious, wealthy young man comes up to Jesus to have a discussion about what it takes to gain eternal life:

> Just then a man came up to Jesus and asked, "Teacher, what good thing must I do to get eternal life?"
>
> "Why do you ask me about what is good?" Jesus replied. "There is only One who is good. If you want to enter life, keep the commandments."
>
> "Which ones?" he inquired.
>
> Jesus replied, "You shall not murder, you shall not commit adultery, you shall not steal, you shall not give false testimony, honor your father and mother, and love your neighbor as yourself."
>
> "All these I have kept," the young man said. "What do I still lack?"
>
> Jesus answered, "If you want to be perfect, go, sell your possessions and give to the poor, and you will have treasure in heaven. Then come, follow me."

> When the young man heard this, he went away sad, because he had great wealth. (Mathew 19:16-22)

So a rich young ruler comes up to Jesus claiming he can 'get to God' by his own moral merit.

Jesus takes the challenge and engages him to see if he's actually able to be good enough.

We know from later in the text that this rich young ruler has a religious mindset. He's confident he's been keeping the Law exactly as God requires.

He asks Jesus, "What good thing must I do to inherit eternal life?" or in other words. "Which particular Law of Moses is the magic key to eternal life?"

Maybe he's worn out trying to keep all the Laws and looking for a shortcut...*or*...maybe he doesn't want to miss the one law that might be most important.

Before answering the question, Jesus looks at the man and makes a facetious statement about being 'good.'

Knowing no human can be as 'good' as God's standard of perfection, Jesus puts his tongue squarely in his cheek and says, "Why do you ask me about what is good? There is only One who is good. If you want to enter life, keep the commandments."

"Which ones?" the young man inquires, confident he's up to the challenge.

D: The boy obviously missed the facetiousness.

S: I'd say so.

At this point, Jesus whips out a checklist to measure the boy against: "You shall not murder, you shall not commit adultery, you shall not steal, you shall not give false testimony, honor your father and mother, and love your neighbor as yourself."

"All these I have kept," the young man says with confidence, probably excited he's doing well. "What do I still lack?"

And Jesus doesn't even snicker. Or if he did, Matthew didn't mention it in the text.

Instead, Jesus answers, "If you want to be perfect, go, sell your possessions and give to the poor, and you will have treasure in heaven. Then come, follow me."

The text tells us, "When the young man heard this, he went away sad, because he had great wealth."

D: I've heard this is about materialism. That this man's love of materialism is what stood between him and following God. And in the end, sadly, he chose his possessions over God.

S: Yes, I've heard that too. But I don't think that's the point.

By going through the checklist, in Matthew 19:21 Jesus basically says, "If you expect to get to God by following the Law, then there is always something else. While maybe you've been able to keep a lot of the Law, there's always going to be something you haven't done, something else you haven't been doing.

Jesus says, "I can go all day on this, naming more and more laws until we come to one, or many, that you haven't kept. Because what is required by God is perfection. Eventually we'll get to extremes, such as have you chopped an arm off yet? Or a leg? Things like that." (*my paraphrase*)

But it only took seven commandments until the man came to one he couldn't, or wouldn't, follow.

Jesus challenged him this way: "Can you throw everything to the wind and trust God to fully take care of you if you give up all control? Give up everything you look to for security? Are you willing to trust God perfectly?"

No, the man couldn't. That was too much.

So to sum up, on the one hand, we have the Unmerciful Servant ending up in God's torture chamber. On the other hand, we have the beat-down of a rich young ruler.

In each case, was Jesus being cruel? What was Jesus actually intending? And what does it all mean for us as believers today?

First, Jesus' intention was to teach the Law to those under the Law.

Second, we now are to live in total relaxation and excitement that Christ came and lived a perfect life so all humans can skip the whole process of moral striving (Romans 10:4, Galatians 5:1).

Therefore, we must conclude that the parable of the Unmerciful Servant is not 'a challenge for *us*.'

D: That's good.

S: And again, this is nothing new or different. It's just seeing the flat theological earth as round.

D: By the way, can you explain a bit about the 'new creation' thing? What are you talking about when you mentioned that earlier?

S: That reminds me: I recently heard a well-known

mega-church pastor say to, and of, his congregation: "We're all sinners."

It struck me as odd and got me thinking.

The statement "We're all sinners" was certainly true before Jesus sacrificed himself on the cross and before we identified ourselves with that sacrifice.

Before we became 'crucified with Christ' (Galatians 2:20), we sinned because we were sinners. We had no choice. Remember 'inside/outside' of the cup? Sinning because we were sinners was our identity.

But now, is it correct to say, "We're all sinners?"

Paul didn't think so.

He said we are new creations (2 Corinthians 5:17).

Our identity is no longer as 'sinners.' We still sin, yes, but we are not sinners by identity.[1]

Our very natures are no longer opposed and contrary to God. We are in alignment with God's Spirit now, and God's spirit lives in us and through us.

D: So if that's true, why do we still commit sins? Why don't we act morally perfect now?

S: Because of what the Bible calls 'the flesh.' The flesh is not a concept meaning 'sin nature' as translated in a few versions of the Bible. 'The flesh' simply means our physical limitation as finite humans.

If we are to trust in 'the flesh,' we are living in stress and fear and worry that we will not have enough, we will not be provided for, and therefore, we do things to make sure we're looking out for Number One, to meet our own needs first and foremost, even if it's to the detriment of those around us.

But what if we trusted God fully to meet all our needs? Would we need to lie, cheat, and steal to take care of ourselves? What would be the point? God is sufficient to take care of everything for us—we are freed up.

Freed to sacrifice for others, freed to rest knowing that God is looking out for our Number One so we don't have to. We are totally free to look out for everyone else's Number One, knowing that we'll be fully taken care of by God as we do so.

But we still have memories of what it's like to be fully committed to taking care of Number One at all costs.

Let me tell you a story about myself that may help clarify things.

D: Can't wait.

---

[1] By sin, we mean making decisions out of self-protection or self-preservation apart from God.

Scene 14

No Country For Old Thinking

"If I don't figure this place out soon, I will die here!"

I wrote that phrase as my Facebook status after having lived and worked overseas a little more than a year.

It got many responses, many sympathies: "Maybe it's time to come home…"

I appreciated the well-wishes, but what I actually meant by the message was the complete opposite of how everyone back home understood it.

I was talking about a mindset. A mindset I found I could not help but have.

I landed in my new country as an American in a foreign workplace.

The American workplace mindset I brought to this new country was characterized by pressure and stress, with a focus toward maximum work production at all costs every minute I was on the job.

That was how I was trained to think in America. That was how my environment conditioned me to behave. So when I arrived on foreign soil, it was as natural as sneezing. I didn't even think about it.

Now that I was in my *new* country, I found I was under a different set of rules. The pressurized, stressed out, work-at-all-cost mindset *didn't even exist* in my new environment.

I went about my job, often falling into the usual pressurized, stressed-out mindset, thinking: *My boss is not happy with me, I'm not doing enough! I need to be accomplishing more and more and more! Ahhhhh! I'm a horrible employee! I'm going to be fired!*

But, strangely enough, I found that my boss *did not* have that view of me at all. In fact, no one in the office was putting that kind of pressure on me. No one was expecting me to be under that stressed-out, pressurized, work production every-second-of-the-day mindset.

By having that mindset, I was actually *confusing* everyone around me. They couldn't understand my behavior.

When I met with someone in the workplace, I didn't do what was customary. What was customary was to take time to talk about life, family and current events over tea or coffee and only if there was time after that, talk about work.

Instead, they would see me rush in, get what I needed to do my job, and rush off.

They were confused, but no one ever chastised me for it. I found that odd, too. No one even mentioned my strange behavior to me, indicative of a very gracious work place.

Not only that, it seemed they understood that as an American, I was 'that way.' It wasn't hurting them. To them I was only hurting myself. In that regard, they hurt for me.

Every time I put myself under the American mindset of stress and pressure, I found that the only one putting that pressure on me...was me!

So when I posted the status on Facebook, "I am going to die here," I meant I was killing myself by living in my old mindset though I now lived in a new land.

My new environment, workplace, those around me, and the new country I now lived in was not hard and difficult.

No.

It was just the opposite. The only one killing myself, hurting myself by holding fast to the mindset of a country I no longer lived in, was me.

In other words, I lived in a self-imposed jail, one that was not reality. No one was holding me in that jail, especially my boss. I kept myself in there by myself.

And strangely, I lived there while everyone around me lived normally, in freedom. From everyone else's point of view, they couldn't understand why I lived (and thought) the way I did.[1]

What I've described is exactly what Paul describes in Romans 6:3-4: "That is what happened in baptism. When we went under the water, we left the old country of sin behind; when we came up out of the water, we entered into the new country of grace—new life in a new land." (MSG).

We are literally no longer citizens of sin/slavery land. As believers, we are 'new creations.' We literally hold passports as citizens of a new country called 'Freedom Land.'

What is needed is a renewing of the mind (Romans 12:2, Ephesians 4:17; 20-24); to simply understand where we now live.

In my new, faraway country *I* needed to rethink things. *I* needed a 'renewing of my mind.' *I* needed to adjust to the mindset of the country where I now lived, because the old way of thinking was useless to me now.

Not only was it useless, it was harmful to live in the old way of thinking in my new country. An old tyrannical system had been replaced by a new system, a new system of freedom and life and relationship.

And I couldn't believe how good it was! I never thought I could have a work environment that free!

In freedom, I could now relax and do my work with a sense of hard work and accomplishment without the stress and pressure.[2]

Sometime in the future, I may get an opportunity for citizenship in my 'new' country. And if that happens, I'll still remember what it was like living and working in America. I'll still feel the 'natural' tug to put myself under undo stress and pressure. But it will become less and less over time.[3]

After having gained citizenship in my new country, I might be tempted to run back to the United States for other reasons. Maybe I'd be scared of things I might not be able to negotiate in the new country, like the fact they don't collect taxes, or the fact that companies have no retirement funds or unemployment benefits. There are a million ways I might fear I might not be taken care of.

What I've described is exactly what the DOI faced in leaving slavery in Egypt for the Promised Land.[4]

This Egypt/Promised Land picture is no accident. God did it on purpose. And now that Christ has come, we live our Christian lives by resting (a constant 24/7 Sabbath rest) like the inheritance of the Promised Land.

God said to the DOI, "I'm going to take you to the Promised Land and meet your every need, down to the very last detail of your lives, *if* you obey my commands."[5] Not because they 'deserved' this nice treatment (Deuteronomy 7:7-9; 8:18, 9-10), but because God made a promise to Abraham.

Paul, in Romans 6, says the Christian life is like the Israelites moving out of Egypt into the Promised Land, but even better.

Everything is provided for us, but this time, nothing is contingent on our behavior. God's promise holds true because his spirit lives inside us, and he will always take care of himself (2 Timothy 2:13).

We can relax and live in the new land.

And though we live in a new country, we still have a backlog of memories (behavior patterns) from the old country that still haunt us.

All these behavior patterns, every single one of them, boils down to this: Do we trust God with our lives—or not?

Again, Paul says what is needed is not a change in our natures. Jesus changed the very nature of the 'inside of the cup' on the cross (2 Corinthians 5:17). Our very natures are now aligned (in agreement) with God's spirit.

No, what is needed is 'a renewing of the mind' (Romans 12:2, Ephesians 4:17; 20-24 – especially vs. 23). To understand *in our minds* our new identity. To understand our identity as citizens of 'Freedom Land' instead of "Sin-Slavery Land." (Romans 6). To understand that God is entirely trustworthy to meet all our needs and desires.[6]

This is really important: Our minds need to stop thinking of our identity as 'sinner,' and begin to think in terms of what being a 'new creation' means.

And this is not a 'work' we have to do.

We don't have to constantly choose to live in Slavery Land or Freedomland. We don't need to constantly monitor ourselves, always asking, "Which land am I living in today, at this moment?"

That would be falling back into rules and religion.

Paul says freedom land *IS* where we live. Reality is that we reside squarely in Freedom Land.

So live there, Paul urges us—Understand where you live and enjoy it! It's a fact. It's concrete. It will never change.

Jesus + Nothing is fully sufficient for everything.

Every.

Thing.

D: So what other bombshells are you going to drop on me?

S: How about the wanton display of arrogance by Jesus' disciples James and John in Matthew 20:20?

D: I love those guys.

S: The great thing about this brutal display of arrogance is that we often think we must 'clean ourselves up' before God will accept us. And though

Jesus never shied away from telling anyone the truth to their face, neither did he blast these guys for their wanton sin and send them away. He loved them in their naiveté.

As he does with all of us.

The Bible, all the way through, consistently portrays a God that is fair, loving and trustworthy.

D: Even in the Old Testament?

S: Even in the Old Testament.

D: Hmm. I'm not so sure. I gotta hear this!

---

[1] This can be seen in 2 Corinthians 6:11-13 (MSG)

[2] The analogy breaks down, as all analogies eventually do at some point, because I can and should 'work' hard at my job. But in our Christians lives, we are told to 'rest' in our inner spirits as we piggy-back on God's spirit doing his work in his power. There is a subtle, but huge difference there. We partner fully with him, never ever doing any of God's work in our own effort. We wait for him to give us the plan then do it in his strength. It's really a great way to live. I've been doing it for some time now, and I love it.

[3] I am not disparaging the American work culture. America has enjoyed its day in the sun as a superpower for many decades, testifying to the value of an ethic of hard work.

[4] They were free, but as they wandered in the desert, they often (all too often) pined for the security of slavery in Egypt, and wanted to go back. They wanted security and safety over following God by faith on a moment by moment basis. That was too scary for them, as it also seems too scary for most of us. Following rules and rituals (controllable idols) is much easier than following an uncontrollable, live, infinite, and therefore very scary, Spirit. So if we are going to do so, then the question is—is this unpredictable and 'scary' Spirit good

and trustworthy? Or just the opposite? (That is where John 3:16 comes in.)

[5] The Law was a contract where God said, "If you do this, I will do that." But the new system, the one taught in the New Testament, is a new covenant. This means the conditions only apply to God (God made a promise to himself). Nothing we do, or don't do, diminishes any part of God's promises to us to meet our needs (2 Timothy 2:13). Is this 'health and wealth' gospel? No. Because God is wise. He gives us what we need in his timing and in his infinite wisdom. We can trust that.

[6] The legitimate ones, of course, but he's God, he can throw in illegitimate desires too. And I don't mean sin desires, things that hurt us, but if God decided he wants to give someone a Ferrari, who are we to say he shouldn't? After all, I'd like a Ferrari. Wouldn't you? But in most cases when someone like a TV preacher, for instance, says God gave him or her a Ferrari, it probably wasn't really God giving it to them (understatement alert).

130 - /thē·*il*·logical/

-Episode Two-

Freedom!

Paul and Those Crazy Galatians

"I am not a slave (of religion), and I'm on the side of any slave interested in their emancipation."

    —The late atheist intellectual Christopher Hitchens

"It is for freedom that Christ has set us free. Never again let anyone put you under the shackles of slavery."

    —Paul of Tarsus

Scene 15

Give Me That Ole' Testament Justice

S: It's been excellent talking about Jesus and the book of Matthew, and now we're about to blow the house wide open.

D: I feel the theological inconsistencies melting away as we go.

S: Before we go any further, consider this:

Paul did not create a theology from the words and teachings of Jesus. His theology was dictated from the *completed* mission of Christ.

Paul did not struggle with how to live out the Sermon on the Mount. He probably would have heard the stories and all, but would have understood them in their proper context.

Contradictions theologians have struggled with for centuries were not an issue for Paul because he never saw any.

He understood God's purpose was to free him from his religious lifestyle, and it changed everything in his life from top to bottom.

Paul's theology was something I think God had in mind for us from the beginning. A simple, livable theology with an easy yoke and a light burden.

The purpose of Paul's letters were not to contradict Jesus and make everything more difficult for us to live out and understand. Paul's letters were meant to be a place of rest, fulfillment and freedom.

But before we get to what Paul meant by freedom, let's look from God's perspective why there's even a need for freedom.

First we need to talk about *justice*.

D: Hey, hey, hey! Justice? That doesn't sound like fun to me.

S: You don't think talking about sin, evil and God's judgment is fun?

D: You're being sarcastic, right?

S: Yeah. No one likes to talk about God's judgment, but it's necessary to lay that framework to understand where all this is going. But rest assured, I think you'll find it very interesting, and probably not what you're expecting.

D: Nothing you've said so far was what I was expecting.

S: Good. Then let's keep going:

Ever since the fall of humanity in Genesis 3, God's goal has been to heal and restore the intense love relationship lost when humanity declared, "God, I want a divorce."

A radical and final solution would be forthcoming in the person of Jesus Christ (Genesis 3:15), but until then, this intense love found himself having to deal with an unfortunate side-effect of the 'divorce;' Humans now lived in a 'garden of good and evil' of their own making.

And it was the evil part that was most problematic for God, and for us.

And that's where history, under the 'fall of man,' kicks off:

In the Old Testament, we find God in a continual struggle with his love for humanity verses their evil and the existence of a sin barrier separating both parties.

It's not that God was somehow constrained by forces beyond his control to bridge that gap (Isaiah 6:5-7). After all, he's all powerful, he can do what he wants. But for reasons of his own, he chose to showcase his love for all humanity in the act of dying on the cross and rising on the third day in a show of triumph over death and sin.

In this, he answered the question once and for all—Is God good? Is God loving? Does God have our best interests in mind?

Now, contrary to popular belief today, God in the Old Testament did not run around creating chaos (such as destroying Sodom and Gomorrah) because he was angry at their sin and wrong-doing.

No.

For two giant reasons:

1. After the divorce, the world was not *God's*. Humans ruled it. God gave them what they wanted. To be the boss of this world.
2. God stepped into *our* world and destroyed Sodom and Gomorrah on behalf of the *victims* (Genesis 18:20-21).

In his mercy, God did not destroy the two cities until they had degenerated to such a degree that there was only one family of victims that wasn't culpable in the widespread evil.

In other words, he patiently waited to see if the cities would 'repent' (ref: book of Jonah). Repent is a word we hate to hear today, but one that simply means to 'change their minds.' Change their minds and agree with God that what they were doing was evil, come to their senses and stop hurting people.

Now don't get me wrong—God does take sin and wrong-doing very seriously. But he's not an angry, out-of-control brute.

There is very good reason God hates sin and wrong-doing. It's because of the consequences it has in hurting the people he loves. This includes the consequences of the sin on the sinner, and especially the victims of the sin.

In the Old Testament, societies existed that became so immoral—so evil—it was no longer possible for them to turn around (Genesis 6:5;11-12). Societies would actually degenerate to such evil that eventually wrong was considered right. The moral compass had turned completely upside down.

And what happens then?

In the case of several societies in the land of Canaan, people simply victimized each other more and more until they were no longer able to turn things around to right, sound living. These were the cycles of societies God was constantly dealing with in the Old Testament. Societies that practiced such things as burning their children alive on sacrificial pyres to fake gods as a good, right and noble thing (2 Kings 17:31, 2 Chronicles 28:3).

So we see that as far as cities in Old Testament

Canaan, moral degradation was happening on a scale we can't even imagine today.[1]

In the case of Sodom and Gomorrah, the entire city would go out at night seeking someone, anyone, to pull out of their house and mass rape (Genesis 19:4-5). And it didn't matter if it was male or female—everyone was fair game. Oh, and did we catch that? This was done with the participation of the *entire city*.

And instead of people being outraged by this, they were used to it. As used to it as seeing your neighbor down the street washing his car (Genesis 19:6-8).

Yes, that was the actual situation. That was the extent of the moral degradation. And it needed to be stopped.

In the Old Testament, we see that when God stepped in to 'judge' (meaning, in this case, to stop or end something), be it a person or a society or an entire people group, it was always the right thing to do. It would have been something we would've done.

And yes, God, on occasion, ordered genocide on certain societies—all men, women, children and animals were to be wiped out. Completely.

Sound harsh?

D: Even the animals? What could they have done?

S: But again, the evil in these societies was way beyond anything we could imagine today. Way beyond a Hitler holocaust or a Rwandan genocide.

One of the many negative effects of the fall of man is death, disease and decay. And death, disease and decay only spread more death, disease and decay until it's epidemic.

Again, and this is very important, these were by no

means healthy, prosperous and thriving communities. God did not just decide to destroy them because he was an angry, out-of-control ogre.

No.

Like a surgeon has to cut out the infection in order to save the body from gangrene, so God brought severe judgment on certain societies in the Old Testament. But not before waiting a very, very long time, and after much pleading with them to repent, to change their minds, about what they were doing (Genesis 15:16, Genesis 18:16-33, Jonah 1:1-2, Jeremiah 6:6-7).

If you are not sure about this analysis, then ask yourself:

What would be your reaction if you were sitting at home one night watching TV as your son or daughter quietly worked on his or her homework and you got a knock on the door to find the whole city had come to pull your child outside to gang rape them on your front lawn?

What would you think?

Would that be ok with you?

Or should it be stopped?

But it gets worse: When you got up and ran to close and lock the door, they beat it down anyway and stole your child (Genesis 19:9).

And what if they did the same thing on another night, but this time they took your child to the town square to be burned alive as a sacrifice to a fake god?

How would *that* sit with you?

If you think these examples are ridiculous, then realize

that there were actual people at an actual point in history who had to face this (Genesis 19).

You would probably want it stopped.

And so did God.

So he stopped it.

He did the right thing.

Today we speak of God's love on one hand, and God's justice on the other. For example, we sometimes hear the God of the Old Testament was an angry God of justice, but Jesus was a God of love in the New Testament.

But the examples I gave above should help us understand that God's justice and his love are not separate concepts. His love and justice are the same thing. The two concepts are married, fused together, inseparable.

God loves the victims, so he must stop (judge) the violence, and those perpetrating the violence.

God loves a victim in his justice wherever one is found.

So we see that quite different from what most of us have always heard, God is always the hero of the Old Testament and never the bad guy.

Why?

Because, again, God was, is, and always will be on the side of victims.

Even today: Victims of child abuse, rape, colonization, victims of the white male, victims of environmental rape, sex-trafficking, etc, and on and on and on.

That's right.

God is always on their side. Always has been, always will be.

So ironically, the God that we generally love to hate is actually the biggest, most powerful ally for victims' rights advocates.

D: Yeah, there seems to be a great deal of agreement that God was a complete unjustifiable monster for destroying Sodom and Gomorrah, and other genocidal examples in the Old Testament, and therefore, he's a terrible God we should have nothing to do with.

S: Yes, I've heard that too, and believed it myself at one time. But then when I saw how Love and Justice work in tandem, it made more sense to me. I hope the most calloused and cynical among us could agree that city-wide gang-rape should instill a little bit of justified indignation in the Lord of perfect love and justice. But again, be that as it may, this is not the reason God destroyed those cities.

Now, for those of us who are, or were, victims of violent crime and have cried out to God for help, but he was silent and didn't show up to stop it, we might legitimately ask: Why did he do nothing?

D: That's a great question.

S: And it has a simple answer. We humans can't have it both ways. And that is the problem.

D: What do you mean?

S: We must ask ourselves: Do we want God to immediately intervene and stop every evil before, or as, it happens? Or not?

When God did step in and stop evil, as in the case of

/thē·*il*·logical/ - 141

Sodom and Gomorrah, we call him a monster. But if he doesn't help us in the midst of being attacked in a violent crime, we say he doesn't love us.

Can we see how we can't have it both ways? That we are unfairly handcuffing God?

And here is something else to consider: If God's goal were to stop every crime before, or as, it happens, then he wouldn't have created the world at all to begin with. He would have stopped everything before it began.

So he must have a different purpose in mind for all this (Isaiah 55:8-9).

And we must also keep in mind that this is not God's world. Things are not as God intended them to be.

This is mankind's world, under human authority, under the rebellion of humans against God.

God is in control of everything, yes, and has absolute sovereignty in the universe, yes, but he is not the ruler of this world. It's not his world.

Yes, Jesus did usher in the kingdom of God by his death and resurrection, but that kingdom exists side-by-side with the natural human world where crime and evil still persist. At the same time, God's love and justice always reigns in God's kingdom (Matthew 13:24-30; 46-43).

So which do we want? God's kingdom, or our kingdom?

D: This is good stuff to consider.

S: Is it making any sense?

D: Yes, it seems that when people criticize 'the God of the Old Testament,' they're not really understanding the circumstances of events in that time period.

S: I agree. I often hear criticisms based on inaccurate understandings of the Old Testament.

D: Ok, give me some more 'justice' talk.

S: You want more? Not tired of it yet?

D: Nope. Bring it.

S: Ok, let's consider this angle:

Recently in Norway, a trial concluded for a man who went on a shooting rampage several years ago, killing 77 people before it was all said and done.

And he was sentenced to 21 years in prison.

21 years?

Not even a year for each person he killed.

Is not a life worth more than a year? At least, is it really worth less than a year?

What was worse was the interviews with victims' families and people on the street after the sentencing.

One man said, "I want to put that man in a room and yell at him for twenty minutes. Just yell at him...No, maybe for a half an hour..."

Yell at him?

One of the victims' mothers was excruciating to watch. You knew she wanted to condemn the bastard to the depths of hell, spitting every invective she could from her mouth.

But through tears she flip-flopped like a living

pancake.

The interviewer asked, "Was the sentence enough?"

"Well, I guess it was," she sheepishly answered, not sure if she could say anything in judgment against another human being.

"But my daughter," she continued, "we still can't get what happened out of our minds....but the court did the right thing...but the memory of her lives with us every moment...but we respect the court's decision...and yet..."

It doesn't translate well in my retelling, but believe me, she was torn in two between her spirit and intellect.

How do we explain this?

Because the West loves the love of God, but not his justice. One of the worst 'sins' in the world today is to 'judge' others.

So maybe this is the great Scandinavian experiment: If we agree to stop judging others, maybe we'll no longer be judged. Because if we say others deserve God's justice, maybe that means we deserve God's justice as well.

I wonder how this 'experiment' will turn out in the long run?

Societies will continue to grapple with how to organize systems of justice and punishment, but what about *our own* culpability and sin and wrong doing that *we do* every day in the form of gossiping about co-workers, belittling our spouses, stepping on people to get ahead, back-biting and talking behind others' backs at parties and on the phone with friends?

D: Yeah, you're right. Not many of us are murderers,

but none of us are perfect. So what's the solution to living in constant fear of God's retribution and rejection for *our* wrong-doing against others?

S: Glad you asked. And it all centers around Jesus Christ's death on the cross and resurrection from the dead.[2]

The Bible declares there's a better way of dealing with our human evil and wrong-doing. It's by leaving all this keeping tabs on sin and evil—all this 'judgment' stuff—behind.

God relegated it to the *Old* Testament, where he left it 2,000 years ago for a better, more complete, more comprehensive solution. The solution was to focus and cast all judgment on himself in Christ's death on the cross to pave the way for God to live inside his community of believers.

And now Paul, the famous apostle Paul, is going to tell us exactly what this death of Jesus on the cross, and his subsequent raising to life again, means for us as believers.

---

[1]And today, incredible evil is done mostly in secret until the person is caught, or at the very least, public evil is done in the wake of worldwide condemnation.

[2]We've all heard this story many times, so I won't repeat it here. But please refer to Matthew 26-28, or Mark 14-16, or Luke 22-24, or John 18-21.

Scene 16

Are We All a Bunch of Crazy Galatians?

S: Now we're getting to where Paul is going to explain how Jesus' death on the cross unlocks freedom for us. Let's just dig straight away into one of the greatest books in the Bible. It's always been a favorite of mine. Now even more so.

D: Bring it.

S: Paul gives an introduction of himself to the early Christians in chapter one. Probably a good idea, since he was once involved in carrying out a pogrom against this new 'Christian' sect. Yes, Paul, our beloved Paul, was happily well on his way to being a genocidal mass-murderer before he met Christ.

D: Ouch!

S: But it's true. As Paul himself stated at the end of 2 Corinthians 2, "We do not water down the gospel to make it more palatable. We speak the truth" (*my paraphrase*).

Consider this: Last time I was in London, I didn't see St. Hitler's Cathedral. Oh, wait. That's because there isn't one.

Nor did I grow up down the street from St. Pol Pot's Elementary School of the Killing Fields for Little Boys and Girls. Or St. Mao Tse Tung's University for the Eradication of All Intellectuals.

These simply didn't exist.

What did exist down the street from me, however, was St. Paul's Elementary School. And what I did see smack in the middle of London is St. Paul's Cathedral. This unbelievably amazing cathedral was constructed by much sought after genius architect Christopher Wren.

D: Wow.

S: That's right. The power and greatness of God stares at us from the name on these two buildings—St. Paul.

But we have to ask ourselves: Was Paul great?

Because here's the undiluted truth: God chose a genocidal maniac to show us how great God is (1 Timothy 1:15-16).

D: Huh?

S: Paul, who once was on a murderous, genocidal rampage, after he embraces Jesus, is now seen crying over a letter to the Corinthians with a soft and tender heart (2 Corinthians 2:4).

D: Wow! That's amazing!

S: But he'd be the first to tell you he was the 'foremost of sinners' (1 Timothy 1:15-16, Ephesians 3:8, Titus 3:3-7).

Worse than Hitler?

Yes.

Worse than Pol Pot?

You bet.

Worse than Andrew Jackson?

Yes.

Worse than Saddam Hussein?

Uh huh.

We see the power of God is displayed glaringly in the jar of clay that was Saul (later Paul) of Tarsus. And we should be nothing short of jaw-droppingly amazed that an elementary school and a world-renowned cathedral, among thousands of other buildings around the world, bear his name.

When we view Paul's life the same as the early Christians, we can come to no other conclusion than the greatness of God; of God's power to change people's lives 180 degrees from where they were headed (1 Timothy 1:15-16).

S: Ok, chapter one of Galatians: Completed.

D: Admirably.

S: Ha! Thanks. Let's jump right into chapter 2:

> We who are Jews by birth and not 'Gentile sinners' know that a man is not justified by observing the law, but by faith in Jesus Christ. So we, too, have put our faith in Jesus Christ that we may be justified by faith in Christ and not by observing the law, because by observing the law no one will be justified. (Galatians 2:15-16)

There it is. Hits the nail on the head, doesn't it?

D: Wow.

S: Let's look at this next collection of verses in rapid-fire succession: In verse 17, we do not 'try to be good.' In verse 19, Paul says, 'I tried working my butt off and keeping rules to please God, but it didn't work.' And in verse 20, he informs us of a very revolutionary notion: "I've completely identified myself with the act of Christ's crucifixion, and it is no longer *I who live*, but *Christ lives in me.*"

D: Powerful.

S: He keeps going in verse 21 by saying, "To go back to rule-keeping would be to abandon my freedom in Christ. So I refuse to do that; I refuse to repudiate God's grace (cross reference Hebrews chapters 6:4-8 and 10:19-39). Because if being set right with God could be accomplished by rule-keeping, then Christ died needlessly."

D: This is very clear. Paul is making your job easy.

S: Then I'll just keep out of the way and let Paul The Master Theologian do his thing, which leads us straight to chapter 3, one of the greatest chapters in the Bible.

Paul is astounded that the Galatians are doing two things horribly wrong:

First, they are mistakenly thinking they are initially reconciled to God (what we commonly called 'saved,' or 'salvation') by keeping the Law, or moral rule-keeping (Galatian 3:2).

And second, they are mistakenly thinking that after they are 'saved,' they live their lives with God each day by following the Mosaic Law, or a law, or laws, or by moral rule-keeping in general (Galatians 3:3).

Let's break this argument down and look at it carefully:

Verse 2: "Did you receive the Spirit by observing the law, or by believing what you heard?"

Verse 3: "After beginning with the Spirit, are you now trying to attain your goal with human effort?" (also refer to Colossians 2:19)

We know we became 'saved' simply by believing that Christ's death and resurrection on the cross applies to us personally, and being identified with that is what makes us 'right with God' (Galatians 2:20).

But what about everyday living after that?

Let's look at this passage of scripture from John 6:60-66:

> Then many of his disciples, when they heard these things, said, "This is a difficult saying! Who can understand it?" When Jesus was aware that his disciples were complaining about this, he said to them, "Does this cause you to be offended? Then what if you see the Son of Man ascending where he was before? <u>The Spirit is the one who gives life; human nature is of no help!</u> The words that I have spoken to you are spirit and are life. But there are some of you who do not believe." (For Jesus had already known from the beginning who those were who did not believe, and who it was who would betray him.) So Jesus added, "Because of this I told you that no one can come to me unless the Father has allowed him to come." After this, many of his disciples quit following him and did not accompany him any longer. (John 6:60:66—New English Translation, *underline mine*)

Look closely at verse 63, the underlined sentence. Jesus himself is pretty clear: "The Spirit is the one who gives life; human nature is of no help!"

In Galatians 3:2, Paul asks them again about salvation: "Did your new life begin by working your butt off for God?" (MSG, *my paraphrase*)

The rhetorical answer is emphatically: *No.*

Taking it a step further, moving from 'salvation' to living our everyday lives with God, he states in Galatians 3:4: "Only crazy people would think they could complete by their own efforts what was begun by God."

In other words, does God work in your life because of your moral striving[1]—by reading the Bible regularly, by praying regularly, by serving people regularly, by keeping a regular 'quiet time'? Or because you trust him to do everything in and through you?

The answer is pretty clear in 3:10—Anyone who tries to live by his own effort, independent of the power of God, is doomed to failure.

What he describes is living the Christian life as a 'religion.'

And Paul says don't do it.

Continuing to Galatians 3:11, Paul says no one can sustain a relationship with God by rule-keeping independent of God. The Christian life is lived by faith and trust in what God is doing for us. "The person who lives in right relationship with God does it by embracing *what God arranges for him.*" (MSG)

Paul means this for every day, all the time. Not just when we 'come to God' in our one-time 'salvation' decision.

How did we receive Christ? By no effort of our own. How do we live each day with Christ? By no effort of our own.

After this one-time 'salvation' decision, we tend to think we should do things for God as a pay-back, or as a sacrificial offering of gratitude (usually stemming from a misunderstanding of Romans 12:1).

All this sounds good and pious, but Paul says it's deadly.

Because once we succumb to self-effort, it's 'religion.'

And Jesus is *not* a religion.

There is no room for 'religion' (self-effort of *any* kind) in our lives with God.

So don't give up your *freedom* by making Jesus a *religion*, Paul says.

D: Wow, that's deep.

S: Yeah, and I think we as the 'historical Christian church' may have badly missed the mark on this one.

D: How so?

S: It's been traditionally taught in Protestant theology that yes, we come to God by what he arranged for us (Christ's sacrifice), but then we live out the Christian life 'by grace.' And living 'by grace' has meant that we try (to 'be good' or 'serve God'), but we make mistakes (sin), so therefore we are to confess these sins to others, then we repent at the foot of the cross, come back to God, then go out and try to be morally good again as we serve God.

And when we fail again, the cycle repeats itself. And our participation in these cycles is taught as a *good* thing—a process called 'sanctification'—where over time, our 'outer man (or sin nature)' is being destroyed as we grow and mature toward perfection, 'Christlike,' which has been the traditional goal of the Christian life.

No.

After Jesus' death and resurrection, we were never intended to live this way.

Remember the context of this part of Galatians. The context is our day in and day out relationships with God. And we see from Paul that, just as it was with 'salvation,' it's *always and continually* what God *arranges for us.*

Always.

Never what we 'do' for God.[2]

This line of reasoning keeps going in verse 12—Rule-keeping and moral striving in our own power independent of God never results in a free life of faith with God.

Never.

But let's say, just for the sake of argument, that we want to live by rules and rituals and are able to keep some of the rules.

Well, Paul says that if we choose to live this way, it only results in having to constantly keep the rules, and never leads to freedom and abundant life (Romans 10:5).

We see clearly in Galatians 3:13-14 that on the cross Jesus absorbed into himself all sin and rule-keeping so that we are now able to receive God's life, God's very spirit, simply by believing that this plan of God's is right and good. We do this by faith, agreeing with God that his plan is good and right (theme of the entire book of Hebrews).

> Christ redeemed us from the curse of the law by becoming a curse for us, for it is written: "Cursed is everyone who is hung on a pole." He redeemed us in order that the blessing given to Abraham might

come to the Gentiles through Christ Jesus, so that by faith we might receive the promise of the Spirit. (Galatians 3:13-14)

S: Ok, for the rest of chapter 3, Paul tells us of the unbelievable good news that we are now heirs of God's inheritance in his 'will,' the original promise to Abraham.

D: How cool is that!

S: Very cool.

We see that the Law was an addendum to keep the DOI on course until the promise came to bear.

Paul is saying the Law has nothing to do with the promised inheritance—the inheritance believers receive as children of God. The Law was merely a tutor to keep the DOI on track, to protect them from moral danger and distraction for a period of time until the Messiah came. "The purpose of the law was to keep a sinful people in the way of salvation until Christ (the descendant) came, inheriting the promises and distributing them to us" (Galatians 3:19-MSG).

As the descendant, Christ is the inheritor of all of God's promises. And all this applies to us as everything that applies to Christ also applies to us (Galatians 2:20).

So everything pertaining to inheritance and promises has nothing to do with the Law, Paul says. Inheritance and the promises of God is the endgame. The Law was merely a pawn in the action.

Now here's the most important part of chapter 3:

Galatians 3:25-27 states, "Your baptism into Christ was not just 'washing you up for a fresh start.'"

In other words, we do not start by 'accepting Christ' (salvation) and then live in cycles of sin-repentance-grace, sin-repentance-grace, as we *work out* our salvations in fear and trembling.

That's not it.

The book of Galatians clearly states that we don't *work out* our salvations in our own power apart from God any more than we initially came to God that way (Galatians 2:20, first part of chapter 3).[3]

In fact, our own effort and power never comes to bear in anything as far as our relationship with God is concerned.

It's all God.

Anything added is 'religion.'

All his plan, all his power, all his strength, and none of ours, all the time, for our whole lives (Matthew 11:28-30).

So we are not washing ourselves up for a 'fresh start,' but we are 'clothed with Christ'—which means we are fully identified with Christ's life, which is the fulfillment of God's promise to Abraham.

So Christians looking toward the goal of 'becoming Christlike'—Congratulations, you made it! You're there! (Galatians 2:20)

Now, though we are 'there'—the perfect Christ lives in us and through us—we see that we still have bad behaviors.

So what's the deal, Paul?[4]

Paul's answer to the 'sin' problem—the fact that we still have bad behaviors—is to 'always live in the Spirit, and you will not carry out the desires of the flesh.' (Galatians 5:16)

In other words, live your identity as being fully identified with Christ and his spirit that lives inside you.

It's that simple.

D: But what does that look like?

S: Somehow I knew you were going to ask that.

It looks like this: That God's strength is made perfect in our weakness (2 Corinthians 12:9-10). In other words, as we go about our lives in our 'jars of clay,' people see God through and in us because God is automatically there. And the goal is God loving people through us, not us loving people in dependence on God (Galatians 5:6).

S: Can you see the subtle difference?

D: I think so.

S: We can be the biggest 'sinner' in the world and God can still love people through us. Isn't that amazing?

D: Yes, it is.

S: And God wants other humans around us to be amazed by this.[5] That's God's strength made perfect in our weakness.

So to be clear, our jars of clay are *not* slowly being broken down in a process of sanctification. We have the same 'jar' throughout our whole lives.

The goal isn't to perfect ourselves. The goal is that the perfect God lives in and through us, and we simply allow God's Spirit to be who he is as we live our lives with God each day.

As God's children, we are new creations (2 Corinthians 5:17), no longer with a sin nature that needs to be broken down (Romans 5 and 6).

D: You're saying we as believers no longer have a sin nature?

S: That's correct.

D: But what about Romans 7, where Paul is clearly struggling with his sin nature?

S: I just knew you were going to bring that up...

---

[1] "God helps those who help themselves"—Though a saying commonly thought to be in the Bible, this phrase was actually made popular by Benjamin Franklin in the 1700s. Franklin (a Deist) believed in God, but did not believe God intervened in human affairs. Thus all action for good and for change falls in the realm of human effort and responsibility.

[2] But what about the verse that states that at the end of our lives, God will give us a pat on the back saying "Well done good and faithful servant!"(Matthew 25:21,23 and Luke 19:17). First of all, I would argue there's a better interpretation of this parable than what's been traditionally heard and taught (see Part 4 of this book for a discussion of Matthew 25). But taking the traditional interpretation at face value for the moment, let's ask: 'Well, if we are servants, then what is the Master asking us to do?' The Master (actually Jesus, not the 'master' of the parable) is clearly not asking us to live lives for God in our effort. So what is he asking us to do? He is asking us to rest in our inner spirits, get out of his way, and let him do everything for us. We are not to work for him (John 6:29, "Jesus answered, 'The work of God is this: to believe in the one he has sent.'"), but just live our normal lives in freedom and let God's spirit work in us and through us, and watch the miracle of God's strength made perfect in our weakness (2 Corinthians 12:9). (And this

is not weakness = sin, but weakness = our physical, finite beings, what Paul calls 'jars of clay,' which again, is not sin, or sin nature, but merely our physical selves on earth.) Along similar lines, didn't Christ commission all believers to "Go therefore and make disciples of all nations...."(Matthew 28:18-20) Isn't this a work we're supposed to do? No. It's important to understand that Christ gave this commission, but also told the disciples (and the first community of believers) to stay in Jerusalem and wait. They were to do nothing but wait until the Holy Spirit came. And then, when the Holy Spirit came in Acts 2, they were simply to follow God's lead. The community of believers, the early church, piggy-backed on the strength, guidance and work of the Holy Spirit, not their own work and effort in accomplishing the commission of Matthew 28. But then we might ask: "That was the book of Acts—What about us today? We don't see the Spirit work like this, in our midst, anymore. So what do we do?" Answer: Is God's spirit silent today? Does he really not guide us and communicate with us directly anymore? Really? If that is what we think—and it's certainly been my experience for most of my life and for many people I know—then we need to wait. We need to wait on God. That is what Jesus asked the early church to do. Stop all your activity and busy-ness and wait. And you will find that he will and does show up. But the timing, the guidance and power are his, not ours. We can be busy. We can get ahead of God. We can run around all we want. But if we want to see God, if we want to do God's work with God, and not in our own exhaustion and burn-out, then we need to wait for him and his timing. Our job is to wait. And then we will see God. That is how the Christian life is supposed to be lived.

[3] What it means to 'work out our salvation' is explained in Colossians 2:6-7.

[4] This is usually the point where we think the answer is that we need to be in cycles of trying to be good-fail-repentance-accept God's grace and doing it over and over as the 'outer man' is chipped away and Christ inside us shines through more and more (sanctification) as we approach perfection in our actions and behavior, which is to be 'Christ-like.' But is that correct? Seems that the truth is that we are fully identified with Christ who lives in us right now. Christ does live his life in us and through our faulty limited jars of clay

right now, in his fullness and life.

[5] Paul makes it clear—we do not conclude that sinning more makes God more visible. That is not the point. Sin happens enough without putting extra effort into it. God is glorified through us as we simply be ourselves, no more, no less. (See Acts 5—Peter told Ananias, "You didn't need to fake people out. You could've just been yourself.")

Scene 17

I Misinterpret When I Don't Want To, And Want To Misinterpret When I Don't Try To

---

D: So what about Romans 7? Where Paul is clearly struggling with his 'sin nature'? Doesn't that contradict what you're saying about us as believers no longer having a sin nature?

S: This is how I think we're supposed to understand the second half of Romans 7, where the situation of Paul struggling with his sin nature occurs: The audience of the book of Romans was a mixture of converted Jews and Gentiles, but for almost the entire book, Paul is addressing ex-Jews and their concerns with how this whole Christian thing (Jews and Gentiles together) works.

Paul makes the argument in chapters 5, 6 and the beginning of 7, that sin and death were killed off by Christ and we are no longer slaves to sin. That our identity is no longer as sinners because we have been made a new creation (2 Corinthians 5:17).

Then he gives an object lesson contrasting two ways of life; trying to 'get to God' by living under the Law vs. living identified with Christ as a new creation.

He is putting out the challenge: Here are two mutually exclusive ways to live. Decide for yourself which is better; which one makes more sense.

As I mentioned, in Romans 5, 6, the first part of 7, and all of 8, Paul shows what it's like to stop striving and live in Christ under Christ's finished work for us. In the second part of Romans 7, he shows what it's like if we don't go that route and choose to deal with our sin natures under the Law apart from Christ.

So this famous Romans 7 passage about Paul struggling with sin is actually Paul in his natural self before coming to Christ, and how inadequate it is to try to live a moral life (to get to God, or to please God) under the Law apart from God's help and intervention (Christ).

Paul's conclusion, in chapter 8, is that instead of living and struggling under the Law in the natural self, the best way to live is to come to Christ and live in freedom under the finished work of Christ in the power of the Spirit.

Why continue to struggle in failure with a sin nature when you can be outfitted with a new nature for free, one that is free from sin right now?

Jesus' inside/outside the cup analogy has come to fruition. The inside of the cup is changed at 'salvation.' Your very nature is changed. You are a 'new creation.'

D: So the struggling with sin part of Romans 7 was never meant for us believers?

S: Correct.

D: Because Romans 7 is a picture of Paul struggling with his sin nature before he came to Christ.

S: Yes.

D: So if for centuries people thought this passage was meant for Christians, maybe this is where fatal errors were inserted into 'sin' theology?

S: I think so.

D: Wow, this is great stuff.

S: So we see in the book of Galatians that between us and God, the goal isn't our own perfect moral behavior. The goal is God himself loving others through us (John 13:34). Not us loving others in our own power apart from Christ, but resting in Christ (Matthew 11:28-30) as God loves people through us. The distinction is subtle, but it's vitally important that we get this.

D: Well, having God love others through me as I sit back and rest in my spirit sounds much more inviting than trying to do it myself.

S: Yes, it's an easy burden to bear for those of us worn out from thinking we have to strive to be good.

D: Is there more about this in Galatians?

S: Yes. Paul keeps this theme going through the whole book just like the Energizer Bunny.

In Galatians 4:4-7, we see that we are an heir to God's life (the inheritance). The Law was slavery, but Christ 'set us free to experience our rightful heritage.'

S: Let me ask you: Is there any mention of effort on our part in that statement?

D: None that I can see.

S: This passage is telling us God did it all. We are now free. We are now nothing but free to enjoy the inheritance as fully adopted children of God. Not as slaves, but as children of God. Full heirs with Christ with complete access to the inheritance. And right now! It doesn't start later, but right now.

D: Wow, that's good.

S: Ok, I'll keep going:

Galatians 4:18 states, "It is a good thing to be ardent in doing good, and not just when I am in your presence."

D: So Paul does tell us that we need to 'be good'?

S: 'Doing good' in this passage means concern for the message—sticking with the message of freedom Paul taught them.

He is not talking about doing good deeds, or being good. He is saying to stick with the message of freedom from all 'trying to be good in our own effort.'

Leave it behind. It's no good.

The message is Christ + Nothing, especially not adding our own effort. We are never to do this.

For the rest of chapter 4, Paul discusses slavery and inheritance, which is self-explanatory.

But then, in chapter 5, Paul drops the bombshell of all bombshells.

BAM! Chapter 5:1 – "It is for freedom that Christ has set us free. Stand firm, then, and do not let yourselves be burdened again by a yoke of slavery."

D: I think you said earlier this would be a great thesis statement for the New Testament.

S: Yes, I think no other verse better sums up what the Christian life was meant to be.

D: I can see that.

S: So to continue on in Galatians 5, we see laid out before us Paul's version of the 'normal' Christian life:

First, verses 2-6 parallel Hebrews 6 and 10, where he's imploring his audience not to throw away the free life Christ sacrificed his life on the cross to give us.

Then in 5:13, Paul says it is absolutely clear that God called you to a free life. But freedom without limits is no longer freedom—it's anarchy, chaos and harm, which is the opposite of love. Use your freedom to serve one another in love, that is how freedom grows.[1]

D: Yes, Paul commands us in verse 14: "Do not use your freedom to indulge the sinful nature, rather serve one another in love. The entire law is summed up in a single command, 'Love your neighbor as yourself.'" So according to Paul, when we 'love our neighbor as ourselves,' all selfish sin falls by the wayside. Is that what he's saying in this group of verses?

S: Well, not really.

D: Huh? Why not?

S: Paul is not actually commanding us to 'love our neighbor as we love ourselves.' Paul says in Galatians 5:16: "This is my advice: live *freely, animated and motivated by God's spirit.*"

He says, yes, love one another, but the crucial question is: How is this done? How is it accomplished? We can 'love our neighbor as ourselves' in our own effort, but Paul argues that doesn't get the job done. *Or* we can live by the Spirit, and in so doing, we will not gratify the flesh.

In other words, the spirit of God is able to accomplish what we in our finite selves (the flesh) cannot do, which is to love others as we love ourselves.

We fall far short, but the Spirit, Jesus' spirit, the very Spirit of God, can and will do it when we rest and get ourselves out of the way, letting him lead as the uniqueness of our spirit lives and acts in conjunction with his.

Paul says we can live in our power, or in the Spirit's power.

Which is the best way to live?

D: But isn't this just another law then? Another rule I need to keep? Do I need to worry each moment of the day whether I'm living by the Spirit, or by the flesh? And worse, do I need to point out when I see others are, or aren't, doing it?

S: No. We know we are living by the Spirit precisely when we are *not* worried, or stressed or harassed by paying attention to laws and rule keeping. When we are *resting*, content in ourselves, and simply waiting on God to do anything that needs to be done, then we know we are 'living by the Spirit' instead of living by the flesh.

We're free from self-effort. Free from all effort.

We are free.

Free to live solely in God's power.

Free from others, free from enslavement to sin, free from shackling rules and rituals.

Free to live in God^2, free to see God's life lived through us (Galatians 2:20).

There is no work involved.

This "not fulfilling the desires of the flesh" (Galatians 5:16) is simply a natural result of living in our freedom and resting in God.

If we are still uncertain about this, turn now to Galatians 6:8—"The one who plants in response to God, *letting God's spirit do the growth work in him*, harvests a crop of real life, eternal life." (MSG)

D: But, I'm wondering: Why doesn't God let us use our effort? What's the big deal?

S: Maybe because of pride?

There is no place for human pride in God's economy (Ephesians 2:8-9).

Humanity rebelled and messed things up causing Rwanda, Darfur, the Crusades, abortion-on-demand, gay-bashing, white male oppression, colonialism, racism, the raping of the environment, the holocaust, the killing and displacement of Palestinians from modern day Israel, 9-11, World War II, Barney the Dinosaur...need I go on?

D: No, I'm good. Thanks. Point taken.

S: I ask you: Has our human 'pride' in any way been shown to be sufficient when compared with God's power and greatness?

I think not.

Personally, I happily abdicate my human pride. I see no use for it, frankly.

D: But what about the upside of human accomplishment? Things like Aids research, Civil rights, The Arab Spring?

S: Well, those are good things, and God upholds the greatness of humanity since we were created in his image (Genesis 11:6). But unfortunately, in the human ruled universe, the bad exists with the good. There is an upside to human accomplishment, yes, but a very harsh downside too. With God, there is *no* down-side. It's *all up*. When we partner with God, great things—the best things—happen.

S: Ok, a slight digression there, but back to our study. Where were we? Oh, living by the Spirit as opposed to the flesh.

D: What is 'the flesh' anyway?

S: Glad you asked.

Now that we as believers no longer have a sin nature, we do still live in the limitations of our physical beings, our 'jars of clay' if you will. We still have needs and worries as to how our needs will be met. Since we aren't God, we're extremely limited in how we are able to meet our needs, and that freaks us out.

The 'flesh' operates simply by choosing to not trust or believe God. We no longer have a 'sin nature' (Romans 6), but we do still contend with the physical limitation of our being, which is neutral.

D: It's not sinful?

S: No. An older translation of the New International Version equates 'the flesh' with the 'sinful nature' in Galatians 5:16-17. But they are not the same thing. An updated version of the NIV translates it 'the flesh.'

Look at it this way: There are three things that most people would be shocked to find existed in the 'perfect' Garden of Eden. And they are work, loneliness, and 'the flesh.'

In Genesis 2:15-18 God invited Adam to work the land and noticed that Adam was lonely.

D: Wait—did you say 'the flesh' was also in the Garden?

S: Yes.

D: How can you say that?

S: Because the flesh is simply the free-will ability to choose. Adam and Eve, in their perfect states, with no sin nature, still had the ability to choose to go against God; to not trust him.

D: Wow, I've never thought of that.

S: We as believers are 'new creations.' When God makes us new creations in the moment of salvation, we do not merely become like Adam and Eve before the fall in Genesis 3. That wouldn't be a new creation, but merely a reverted one.

What we get is better!

We become something entirely new, something never before seen in the history of the universe.

We become a new creation.

Romans 6 explains that we no longer have sin natures (with no choice but to live apart from God's will). However, Galatians 5 is clear that we still have 'the flesh,' which, according to Paul, is simply the ability to choose to live our own way apart from God.

Paul says in Ephesians 1 we have all the power of God at our disposal. God is a perfect friend, a perfect parent, a perfect lover. One who is unlimited in power and resources. So in light of that, in Galatians 5:16-18 he urges us to live with trust in God and not in ourselves (the flesh).

It would be silly to live solely trusting in ourselves (the flesh) when God has taken care of everything for us, and promises to always and for all time provide for our needs. But there still is, and always will be, 'the flesh'—the ability to make our own decisions and do things our own way.

D: So how does all this work practically?

S: Practically, this means that when God says he promises to take care of us, do we believe him? Or do we feel the need to look out for Number One at all costs because if we don't, who will? We worry, beg, steal, kill and lie to make sure our needs are met. But none of this is necessary if we believe God will perfectly provide for us, as he did for Adam and Eve in the Garden of Eden.

And all this leads to Galatians 5:18, where Paul gives the understatement of the book: So why not live by the Spirit, leaving behind the law, self-effort, the 'sin-fail-grace' 'flesh' dominated way of life?[3]

D: Sounds good.

S: Very good.

Lastly, in Galatians 6:11-13 we see that following religion, and living 'religiously' by rules and rituals only and always results in hypocrisy.

Every time.

That religion—all religion—is only good for falseness, fakery, deceit and hypocrisy.

So in conclusion, the message of Galatians is clear—*Do not make Jesus a religion*[4]. If you do, it kills your freedom and kills off your access to the living God. Your own effort only gets in God's way.

Jesus is not about dead rules and rituals.

It's about the living God.

It's life.

It's freedom.

So live in your freedom.

---

[1] This is Paul's picture of the normal Christian life. Not 'sanctification.' Not becoming more 'Christ-like.' Not becoming better behaved. All this is taken care of as we expand our freedom.

[2] Which is what baptism means: To be 'put into.' We are literally put into God's life at salvation. As Paul says, "It is no longer I who live, but Christ lives in me" (Galatians 2:20). I have been put into Christ, just like when Han Solo sliced open the tauntaun and put Luke into it to keep him from freezing in *Star Wars: The Empire Strikes Back*. All that could be seen was the tauntaun, and none of Luke. I am fully identified with Christ. Everything God says is true of him, is true of me, right now.

[3] We see that we don't have to live in cycles of going back to the cross in sadness and repentance. David's contrite heart in the Old Testament is not for us as believers (Psalm 51:17). Contrite hearts were for the DOI who lived 'under the law,' and this included David. David was under the Law. When people lived under the Law, God wanted broken and contrite hearts. People under the Law showed their inner-contrite hearts on the outside by physically wearing sackcloth and ashes. This was an admission to other people and to God that they couldn't meet God's standard of perfection; that they fell short. A broken and contrite heart was an admission to God that, "You're right. I can't do it. I can't live a morally perfect life apart from your help. It just can't be done." Today, we are under a different system. A totally different system. We do not live under the Law. In fact, we 'Gentiles' never have, and never will. The function of the Law being a guide for the consciences of the DOI—the thing that 'pointed them to Christ'—is no longer entrusted to a people group, and most certainly not to be put on the walls of a courtroom (the Ten Commandments). The Law had a specific purpose for a specific group of people, and was a mirror

reflection of the very character of God. We can see that and enjoy it as we read about it in the Old Testament today, but we are not to try to live by it or follow it (book of Galatians). We know within our hearts we're not perfect; that we can't live up to the standard of our own consciences (guilt). Our hearts point us toward the need for a different way to 'get right with God.' We instinctively know we need a legal loophole to 'get right with God,' and in this regard, we—everyone—find that our own 'hearts' point us to the need for Christ (Romans 2:14 (NIV), Galatians 3:24 (MSG)).

[4] This is the same message that is clear in James, Hebrews, Corinthians, and all the books of the New Testament from Acts to Revelation.

Scene 18

The Big Miss

S: Let's look closer at this notion of freedom Paul seems so excited about.

Again, in Galatians 5:1, Paul says, "It is for freedom that Christ has set us free. Stand firm, then, and do not let yourselves be burdened again by a yoke of slavery."

It seems that over the centuries we have burdened ourselves again with a yoke of slavery. We've simply traded the Mosaic Law for our own laws—rules that now govern the Christian life. And to Paul, this is just as bad as trying to follow the Mosaic Law.

We have made laws of reading the Bible regularly, praying regularly, serving others, having a set quiet time, etc, etc. These activities are sometimes referred to as the means by which we grow, and we use them to judge how we, and others, are 'doing' with God.

But Paul says it was never to be this way.

D: Are you saying there is no way to tell good from bad behavior? Are you saying that now Christ has finished sin and death, that everything is arbitrary and willy-nilly?

S: I'm glad you asked that. Because things are not arbitrary and willy-nilly. Under the economy of freedom, Paul gave us one rule in the New Testament as far as sin and behavior goes, and one rule only. This particular rule is not to overshadow the Spirit, as nothing is to ever overshadow the work of the Spirit. But Paul does give us one rule, or guideline, when it comes to behavior.

The one rule I call "The Big Miss." Because it seems Christians, theologians and churches have missed it, and/or misunderstood it, for centuries.

The rule is this simple statement from Paul: "'Everything is permissible for me'—but not everything is beneficial." (1 Corinthians 6:12)

The NASB translation states it this way: "All things are lawful for me, but not all things are profitable."

Paul states this same principle again in 1 Corinthians 10:23: "'Everything is permissible,' but not everything is beneficial."

Paul taught such a degree of freedom in the early churches that they wondered the exact same thing many have wondered down through the centuries: "Hey Paul, if we are *totally free*, and no longer have a 'sin nature' (Romans 5-8, 2 Corinthians 5:17), and God holds no man's sins against him (2 Corinthians 5:19[1]), does that mean we can do anything we want? Are we free to just rip off our clothes and run naked down the street and smoke everything we see and have sex with anything in sight, and *God won't care*? Is that what you're saying, Paul?"

Well......yes, he would respond, and did respond, to those who inquired. That is the meaning of 'All things are permissible.'

D: But doesn't that lead to licentiousness and all out lawlessness? *Think of the children!*

S: Ok, easy now. Calm down. We need to see that there's a second half to the phrase:

Yes, all things are permissible because Jesus died for all sin for all time...*but*...not all things are *profitable*.

Your point about licentiousness is a good one, though, because there was an early community of believers who only heard the first part of Paul's statement and practiced a licentious way of life.

But Jude, one of the little known New Testament writers, wrote a letter to them echoing Paul, "Yes, you *can* live that way, but if you do, you're missing the point." And Jude makes a good argument for a better way to view things, as does Paul.

So, again, in response to the charge that this notion of *freedom* will cause anarchy and rampant immorality, Paul says: "(Yes), all things *are* permissible, but not all things are *profitable*." (*my insert, my italics, my paraphrase*)

So then, what is not profitable?

Simply this: Anything that hurts ourselves or other people.

Simple as that.

D: That's it?

S: Yes.

God does not judge for sin anymore. He's not looking down from above keeping tabs on sin, and hasn't been for 2,000 years.

Ever since Christ died and rose from the dead, we (including *all* humans) *do not sin against God.*

D: Huh? Really?

S: Let me ask you a question: Did God judge Jesus on the cross for Hitler's sins? Were Hitler's sins taken care of by Jesus on the cross, in 33 A.D., at that moment in time? Or would his sins only have been taken care of if and when he embraced God's plan in his heart in some weird retroactive judgment-y way during Hitler's lifetime?

In other words, was Jonathan Edwards correct in his famous sermon *Sinners in the Hands of an Angry God* when he said a dam-burst of the Lord's judgment is being held back against every individual throughout their lifetime until they come to God for salvation, and if they don't, when they die they get a torture blast of God's judgment against them for eternity?

Is that really what the New Testament teaches?

Or is it that Jesus received the dam-burst of God's judgment on *himself* 2,000 years ago?

Isn't it more accurate to say all judgment for the whole of human history's sin was put on Christ at the moment he was on the cross? And therefore, when he rose from the dead, everyone was, and is, forever free from God's judgment for sin?

Doesn't this seem more logical?

No more dams. No more bursting.

D: So are you saying Jesus made it so everyone automatically gets into God's kingdom? Isn't that universalism?

S: Yes, that would be universalism, but I don't think that's what the Bible teaches. Yes, God died to 'take away the sin of the (whole) world.' And yes, there's a lot of evidence that Hitler was an enemy of God if ever there was one. But ultimately it's not our call to make. We just don't know *exactly* how God will deal with it. We know for sure from the Bible that God is just, righteous and fair. He will deal with it in the way he sees fit, and it will be perfect and just however that is. Ultimately, how it's worked out is between him and God, as it is for all of us.

Jesus tells us in Matthew 13 it's not our job to go around pointing out the enemies of God and rooting them out. Jesus said clearly in this parable, and I paraphrase, "That's not your job. It's God's job. Let him take care of it. God says he'll take care of it, so trust that he will. You are to live and let live. You are free. So enjoy your life, and let me worry about my enemies."

D: Wow! *God* said we are to 'live and let live'?

S: Yes, he did. To be clear, obviously we're not talking about *not* telling friends and neighbors about the goodness of God, or *not* loving those who are hurting in isolation or shackled by religion, and simply leaving them alone. No. We have the privilege and the invitation to love *everyone*, regardless of who they are. What Jesus tells us in Matthew 13 is to leave the ultimate *labeling and identifying* of who are God's enemies *to God*.

We live in freedom. Let God deal with those who are ultimately his enemies. It's not for us to identify them, or root them out.[2]

Can we trust him to make those decisions?

D: I would think so.

S: Ok, then, back to the overall discussion:

"Everything *is* permissible," Paul said.

So for the past 2,000 years, and even today, humans have only sinned against each other and against themselves. Not against God.

And this sin against ourselves and others is, and always will be, unprofitable.

We are *free* to pour alcohol down our throats until we kill ourselves.

No one is watching.

We are *free* to look at pornography until we deaden our souls.

No one is watching.

We are *free* to back-bite and gossip until we destroy all our relationships.

The only being in the universe hurt or damaged by these things are us and those around us.

God does *not* hold us accountable. No one goes to Hell for these things.[3]

For those who are a 'new creation,' God never turns his back on them. God never withholds good things from us based on our behavior.[4] What God does for us is never contingent on our plans, actions or behaviors.

There are no contingencies.

His plan to love us 100% keeps going regardless of our actions.

2 Timothy 2:13 says, "If we are faithless, he remains faithful, for he cannot disown himself."

God put his spirit inside us for a very good reason: So

he can keep his promises to himself. Legally speaking, after Christ rose from the dead and we invite God's spirit to live in us, God's promises are binding to himself. The execution of those promises no longer depends on any other party but himself.[5]

So, back to the original discussion, and taking things a step further, if we choose to do something that violates the laws of society (Romans 13:1), or the moral laws of God put in place at creation, we only hurt ourselves and those around us as we are carted off to prison, or find ourselves damaged in some way. But God follows us right into prison, and often chooses to heal us for damage we've done to ourselves in violation of his moral laws, as he's still 100% committed in his love and plans for us.

Paul urges us, in love, to use our free-will to choose to live in love and live 'in the Spirit.' And anything that hurts ourselves or others is unprofitable.

For everyone.

Practicing a lifestyle of intentional evil, and/or living in 'the flesh' (living on our own without God) is not how we were originally designed by God to live. Sin and death is an aberration. It's not how this world was designed to run.

So yes, we *can* do anything we want. But is what we're doing going to get us where we want to go? Is whatever we're doing, or not doing, worth it?[6]

God sent Christ to do a work that started the process of the restoration of all creation. So Paul says it makes sense to get on board with that. Do things that are clearly profitable for yourself and others. Get on board with the grand adventure of life and the excitement of an infinite God who'll always have new things for us to do and experience.

Before you knew Christ, you had no choice but to act unprofitably (sin nature). Now, you've been freed, so use your freedom to act profitably for yourself and others (Galatians 5:13). We are invited, we have the privilege, to live by and discern this 'rule' while living in intimate community with other believers (Acts 4:32-35) under the guidance of the Spirit.

Another question we must ask ourselves is this: Do we think God's living spirit is sufficient to guide us? Is God's spirit, and the counsel of scripture, sufficient to help us discern between loving behavior and unprofitable behavior?

Is God's spirit sufficient to do this without the need to run around judging and condemning each other?[7]

S: Wow, I really got on my soapbox there, didn't I?

D: Yeah, you did. But it was good.

S: So we have this statement: "All things are lawful (permissible) for me, but not all things are profitable." (NASB, parenthesis mine)

What does this *really* mean in practice?

It means this:

When you were a small child and walked into the kitchen, you might have found your mother standing there next to a hot burner on the stove.

You might have looked at the glowing burner with awe and interest. And seeing this, if your mother was being a good mother, she would have said, "Don't touch the burner. It's hot. It'll burn you."

Your mother was being a 'tutor' to lead you to freedom, the exact same way Paul said the Mosaic Law was a tutor to lead the DOI (and through them, all humans) to Christ (Galatians 3:24).

But now let's say you're a grown adult and you go home to visit your family for Thanksgiving. Walking into the kitchen, you find your mother is not there watching; she's in another room talking with family (Galatians 3:25).

You *can* walk over and put your hand on the burner. You are free to do so. No one is watching.

But would that make any sense? Would that be profitable?

Same thing with running into the street.

Right this very second, if you are over age 6, you have complete freedom to run into the street without looking both ways first. No one is watching or policing your behavior.

You have the freedom to do so. All things are permissible.

But would it be profitable?

I think not.

Here is an analogy from a well-known Christian author[8]:

When this author was a teenager, he used to go over the speed limit in his car everywhere he went. Just the *sight* of a speed limit sign made him want to go faster (Romans 7:8-10).

Then one day, he and his father were invited to go to the Indianapolis Speedway and race cars around the track as fast as they could.

Others were going 140, 150, *more than 160mph*, but

our guy, the speed demon, found he couldn't push himself to go over 132mph.

Why?

Because 132 was the limit he felt he could go before the whole endeavor became *unprofitable*. Before it became potentially harmful to himself and/or others.

He felt going faster would be hazardous to his health if he went out of control and smashed into the wall.

So in his *freedom*, he *limited* himself.

No one was watching. No sign or person told him he had to go slower. In his freedom and maturity, he limited himself to avoid unprofitable behavior.

Now the analogy breaks down of course, when we're talking about things like drug addiction, prostitution, child pornography, murder, etc. These are crimes against ourselves and others that in most cases, people have no interest in policing themselves on, so others must intervene.

But as believers, when we talk about unprofitable, unloving behavior towards others—behaviors that aren't necessarily crimes against the state—we live in a community of believers who are in tune with God's loving Holy Spirit to help us discern these matters.

Not to police each other, but to *love* each other.

We can discuss and come to agreement on profitable and unprofitable behavior in love...again, not to make rules so we can go around judging each other, but to live in freedom in the Spirit and to love each other because we are united, or unified, under the strength and guidance of the Spirit.

This is why Paul says—surprisingly in agreement with

today's post-modern thinking—that we are not to judge one another.

However, it's good to have people around to persuade us in love (which is crucially important) as to the damage that could be caused to ourselves and others if we practice harmful behaviors instead of profitable ones[9] (Titus 3:8-9).

D: You know, I was thinking of something that might be off the subject.

S: Ok, jump in.

D: Ultimately, it seems to me humans want to be free from God, free from any moral or behavioral constraints whatsoever. That's what fallen sinful human nature ultimately wants, isn't it? So wouldn't that actually be considered true freedom?

S: Well, it certainly sounds enticing. And it's exactly the appeal the devil made to Adam and Eve in the Garden of Eden. But we must ask ourselves two things: Is being free from God, our creator, really freedom? Is doing whatever we want really freedom? Is that really profitable, for us, or anyone else?

To Paul, this whole thing looks like this: Do we really want to practice the 'freedom' to run out into the street without looking both ways first?

In our freedom, do we really want to indulge in the practice of putting our hand on the stove?

Which is freedom?—Always putting our hand on the stove, or having the ability to exercise our choice to not put our hand on the stove?

Paul looks at this backwards, which is probably how we should see it too.

Before Christ set us free, we had to put our hands on the stove. We had no choice. Our fallen human nature compelled us to do so.

What Christ did when he gave us freedom (Galatians 5:1) was give us the ability to choose *not* to put our hands on the stove.

But we can still put our hands on the stove if we want to, no one is looking,[10] especially not God.

God is *not* policing our behavior.

But yes, he *can* intervene in human affairs if he wants, which will always be his right as, well, God. But mostly, he lets history play out in order to show *us* humans something, not for his benefit or detriment.

D: What do you mean by that?

S: History continues for *us*, in order for God to ask the question, "Ok, you humans rule this world at the moment—How's it going? Do you like what you see? Is everything copacetic? What do you think?"

We blame God for all the ills of the world, but again, this is not God's world. It's ours. He gave it to us under our free will choice when we asked for a divorce.

So what do we think?

Do we like what we see?

---

[1] 2 Corinthians 5:18-19 states, "All this is from God, who reconciled us to himself through Christ and gave us the ministry of reconciliation: that God was reconciling the world to himself in Christ, not counting people's sins against them." This verse has been commonly interpreted to be only pertaining to Christians; those who are 'saved.' But from the context, it is clear Paul is addressing all mankind—all

humans—and not just Christians. Paul crosses from speaking about those who are saved over to the whole world when he says 'God was reconciling the world to himself, not counting people's sins against them.'

² And we're not talking about forming a society where criminal behavior runs rampant. That is not what Matthew 13 is about. It's about how God's kingdom and his people exist side by side with fallen humanity's kingdom, or 'the kingdom of this world.' We can put constraints on societal criminal behavior. We can judge that for sure. But we cannot judge for ourselves who is ultimately in God's kingdom, verses who's an enemy of God. That's up to God.

³ Jesus discusses Hell in the context of following the Law vs. not following the Law. His descriptions of Hell are in the sense of a place or state of being where one doesn't want to be. A state of being or environment that is extremely undesirable. He most likely did not have the 'eternal torture' vision that Dante made popular in Western thinking. Interesting to note also that Hell is not mentioned in the OT. 'Sheol' is a place of unconsciousness, or non-life, after death.

⁴ We do *not* have accountability groups to grow, maintain, help or preserve our relationship with God. We have accountability groups to help save us from the damage we do to *ourselves*, or damage we might be doing to *others*, and for that purpose only.

⁵ When we experience that God is faithful to us even when we're not faithful to him, that is when our faith (trust) in God grows. This is where spiritual maturity happens. As Paul says, 'when we see what God does for us.' It's not, and never has been, what we do for God (Romans 12:3 and Romans 4:14—MSG). Now this begs a question. A very good one. Paul heads it off by rhetorically asking: "Well, if this is true, then shouldn't we sin all the more (our faithlessness) so grace (God's faithfulness) may abound (Romans 5:20-6:23)? Paul says, No. Again, that would be missing the point. First of all, sufficient to the day is the evil thereof..., there's enough evil in the world, we don't need more. But more importantly, if we let sin 'reign' in us, then we become its slave. We voluntarily place ourselves back under shackled slavery.

⁶ It's crucially important that we understand Christ's death freed us *with no strings attached*. Anything less is not freedom. Nor would it be a *gift* (Ephesians 2:8-9). Christ did not die to *demand*, or *force*, that we be loyal to him. He died so we can live in a space of full acceptance by God where we don't *have* to follow him, but we have the opportunity to *want* to. Do we see the difference? In Romans 7, Paul said that the Law did not make people *want* to do the right thing. In fact, it did the opposite. The existence of the Law (or any laws, rules, regulations, or religious system about how to be good, including how the current construct of how the 'Christian life' is to be lived) does not give people the power to live good and profitable lives. Only living by the Spirit does. Living by the Spirit is the answer (Galatians 5:16). But let's look for a moment at the culmination of how Christians have communicated the bottom line of Biblical truth down through the ages. Right now, it seems the church offers everyone on earth only one option—if you want to be identified with Christ's sacrifice, if you want to be 'saved,' you start with the faith decision that Jesus died for you, then you *must* 'follow Christ.' The implication being you must follow Christ to be, or stay, in God's continued good graces, and if not, you have 'fallen away,' you have 'backslidden,' you have 'fallen from grace,' you have fallen out of God's favor (misinterpretations of the parable of the Prodigal Son are used to back this up), or worse, you were never 'saved' to begin with. A good analogy here might help. Many years ago I had a friend who accosted me one November about whether or not I had voted in the United States national election earlier that day. "Did you vote yet?" he aggressively came at me. "You know you *have* to vote. It's what people gave their lives for this country to give you the right to do. They fought and died for your freedom. So you *have* to vote." I calmed him down and responded: "Actually, that's not what freedom is at all. They fought and died so that I would have the right and privilege to vote, or *not to vote*. If they died so I'd be *forced* to vote, that's not freedom. Freedom means I have the choice to do it, *or not*. Either way, I'm still accepted 100 percent as a citizen of the United States. Not shunned, kicked out, or put in jail." That is what it means to live in freedom. I have the opportunity and privilege before me to do something, but my citizenship, my inheritance, my full rights as an adopted son and heir to the king, is not taken away from me if I don't. The greatest fear

someone might have about freedom is that if given freedom, no one would ever vote. But we see over the course of American history that that has not proven to be the case. Yes, it's true, some do not vote. But many do. With freedom comes risk. But giving us freedom is a risk Paul says God was willing to take (Galatians 5:1). Christian pastors, leaders and thinkers fear that if they tell people they can still be accepted by God whether or not they choose to follow him with their lives, *no one* would ever want to follow God. And worse, everyone would just immediately run to rampant sinfulness and moral anarchy. But is this really true? Yes, some might not follow God, and some might go out and deliberately sin. But many *would* follow God. And who are we as humans to decide the risk God took by offering Christ's death on the cross as a *free gift without strings* was not the right course of action? That it was not worth it to God? After all, it's God's risk, not ours. This is the incredibly risky, outrageous, baffling, crazy offer of Good News God has for humankind through the writings of Paul and the New Testament writers. This is what *freedom* means. Therefore, from a position of *freedom*, Paul lovingly tries to persuade us to use our freedom as an opportunity to live for God (Galatians 5:13)—not because you *have* to, but because it's the best way to go about things. Not because you *have* to, but because it makes the most sense. We have twisted Paul's intentions over the centuries to mean Paul is telling us what we *have* to do—as if there is no choice. But if there is *no* choice, then we don't live in freedom. In this case, Christ didn't make us free, and therefore Galatians 5:1 should be removed from the Bible, or what has actually occurred over the centuries is that it will simply be ignored or interpreted away to mean something other than what Paul actually intended. All of what is written in this footnote is exactly why the Bible is *not* a religion. If you asked any random person walking down the street anywhere in the world, "What does it mean to be a Christian?" they would answer "A Christian is someone who follows Christ. Duh." If we followed up and asked, "According to the Bible, can someone want to be accepted by God through Christ's death on the cross and God *will* accept them even though they have no desire to follow him?" The response would be "Of course not. The very definition of being a Christian means you *have* to follow Christ with your life, you *have* to want to follow Christ. You have to be loyal to him." We see by these statements, tragically, that everyone in the world (Christians and non-Christians alike) thinks that Christ died on the cross to force people to follow him. That God is a tyrant who demands loyalty, and if not, you're thrown out in the dark with no hope. We see there is no category for someone wanting to be accepted by God through Christ's sacrifice (and God actually accepting them), even if they don't want to 'live for Christ,' or live the current 'Christian' construct. We must ask ourselves—According to the Bible, is being accepted by God but not wanting to 'live for him' *really* not an option? Can someone know with assurance that Christ died for them—that their identity with God is secure for all time—and yet have no desire to 'live the Christian life'? Can that person still be a fully card-carrying child of God? We must ask ourselves—What is the *true* Biblical position on this?

[7] Most of us need to start further back and ask ourselves: Do we really believe God's spirit is living and active at all, or is it all just a fairy tale? And I'm addressing this to believers now. Especially in the West. We have by and large thrown out, along with the greater culture, the idea of the supernatural. Therefore, what we've been left with is an empty shell of a 'Christian religion' that we follow in our own power because we don't believe we can actually sit back and wait on the power of the living God. So we do it our own way, in our own strength. And it's failing. And not only that, it's unattractive to the entire rest of the non-Christian world. They see through it. They can see it's just another religion we are practicing, so why should they give up Hinduism, Buddhism, Judaism and Islam. Why trade one set of rules, regulations and rituals for another? It makes no sense. And how can we blame them? The real question is: Where is the power? What is reality? Is God really there, and if so, can he communicate to us? Where is the power? I have witnessed in some Islamic societies that in the absence of power in rules, regulations and rituals, some may look to the 'dark' spirit world for power. They know there is power there, and it is practiced and strangely accepted within those societies. The good thing is that they are correctly looking for the 'power.' The bad thing is that they are not finding it in the living God but in the dark supernatural world. And this powerlessness is true for all religions and philosophies of man, even and especially where Christianity is practiced as a religion.

[8] Andrew Farley, God Without Religion

[9] But this should be done among our very close friends and those who know us well. They have earned authority in our lives. They know all the circumstances and this makes a huge difference when discerning the 'behavior' of another person.

[10] 1 Corinthians 6:12, 10:23

Scene 19

Why Can't "Big Brother" Just Leave Me Alone?

D: Ok, so believers are free from laws and rule-keeping and sin and death. Completely free from that.

S: Yes.

D: But playing devil's advocate for a moment, what about someone who simply wants to be free from *all* of this, someone who wants no religion, no God, and just wants to be left alone to swim through life under the forces of evolution?

S: Yes, there are probably some people at this point who'd say, "Well that's all nice, but I don't want God. I don't want rules, but I also don't want to follow God with no rules. I just want to be left alone in my world without religion, without God or the notion of God. Why can't I have that?

D: Yes, what about that?

S: It's a good question and something I sympathize with. I've felt that way many times myself. God knows I haven't always lived without struggle and doubt. In fact, I've lived most of my life in struggle and doubt when it comes to the things of God. It seems like it would be all well and good to simply be left alone.

However, God leaving me alone to myself breaks down

here: In the fact that there are no victimless crimes.

Even when we hurt ourselves and no one else is involved, God still cares about us more than we care about ourselves. And sometimes, in his mercy, he steps in to save us from ourselves.

Practically no one, save for the furthest hermit up in the arctic ice cap, lives in a vacuum. We were created as social beings.[1]

And even if you don't murder someone or participate in child molestation or pornography or drugs, we have to ask: Do you ever gossip? Do you ever back-bite at work? Do you ever complain about the stupidity or incompetence of others, or talk about them in negative ways behind their backs?

Did you do anything today that diminished the dignity of your significant other? Embarrassed them in public? Did anything that made them feel less of a man or woman?

These things may not seem like a big deal to us, but we need to understand they do hurt others.

And God is that person's big brother.

When it comes to God's love/justice (remember they're not separate concepts, but the same thing), the good news is he's fully committed to protecting you from other people. The bad news is he's got that same commitment to protect others from you.

God loves you and is your big brother when others hurt you. But he's also other people's big brother when you hurt them.

Let's take it a step further.

Did you rape someone today?

Probably not, but if you did, would we be ok if that woman's father or brother stood by and did absolutely nothing about it?

Ask yourself, would we call that person loving? The person who stood by and did nothing?

Not only would we call them a horrible person, we might press charges under 'Good Samaritan' laws. And therefore, we have put them under 'judgment.' We have judged that person.

Now why is it considered the right thing to do when we judge someone, but we have a huge problem when God does the exact same thing?

This might be why: Because we think God's judgments are random, or hasty, or don't make sense. But here's all you need to know: God loves you as his little brother or sister, actually, as his own child. And he loves you so much, that when anyone, anyone, anyone, ever, ever, ever does anything—the littlest, tiniest thing—wrong or bad to you, it pisses him off. And he is right there to protect you and defend you by any means possible. He wants to stop it from happening, and show you (and the perpetrator) that what is being done is not acceptable, that the behavior of someone hurting you will not stand. He wants to send you, and the perpetrator, a strong message that he will protect his own. As he should.[2]

Now, if this is the case, why do people rape and get away with it? Why doesn't God immediately swoop down and stop it? Should we rightly ask: Where is God? Yes, we should. And the answer is this: God is not in charge of justice on earth right now. People are. In Genesis chapter 3, humans decided they didn't want to live under God's authority anymore, but to live under their own. And that is the world we live in today. So you could say we got what we asked for.

So what do we think? Do we like what we see? Is the Chernobyl disaster and the Darfur injustice and the Rwanda genocide and oil spills and boiling Middle East tensions and stealing other country's resources and preventing people from having basic needs met because of corporate greed, and Jewish people shoved in ovens, and the little girl being raped by her stepfather night after night that nobody knows about....is this pretty?

Do we like what we see?

This is *our* world. Mercifully, however, we see in the Old Testament that God did not abandon humans totally to go their own way and ultimately destroy themselves. God always stepped into history in judgment to actually try to prevent people from destroying themselves, and others. In Noah's time, they were too far gone. They were destroying themselves at an alarming rate, so God stepped in and put a stop to it all. He placed the rainbow as a sign that he would never destroy people in totality again, but instead he would let things play out and allow people to have all authority on earth. In other words, he'd give us what we asked for, and see how things go. And mostly, even after Noah, people simply went on towards their own destruction, and God would heave a huge sigh. However, God did, at his own discretion, step in and stop the destruction, be it individuals or nations, where the destruction was so bad that he could no longer bear the cries of the victims.

What a different perspective than the one we're used to hearing about God.

So now that the evidence is in, which do we want? For God to be the authority on earth, or for humans to be the authority? Which is best?

Ironically, in the Bible, God set in motion an

experiment where we got to see first-hand what it would be like if God was in charge of justice. He instituted the Mosaic Law, which was all about severe penalties if you didn't perfectly take care of everyone around you. And people hated it! Ironically, they thought it barbaric and wrong. And ironically, people still think the Law in the Old Testament was barbaric and wrong. But mostly because it's impossible for humans to follow the Law, as we see in the four gospels. So in our pride, we lash out at God.

But it's not his fault.

We asked for the divorce.

Luckily, on the cross, while we were yet enemies, he initiated reconciliation. (Romans 5:10, 2 Corinthians 5:17-21)

---

[1] Even if you don't think we were created by God, evolution also clearly attests that we are social beings.

[2] So am I saying that God is busy all day meting out judgments and punishments for everything everyone does to each other in some kind of massive karma-fest? No. God dealt with the evil we all do to each other by having taken the judgment on *himself,* on the cross. That is the mind-blowingly good news of the Bible. Does this erase the consequences and pain and suffering our evil causes? No. Consequences still play out. But our *ultimate* culpability, our responsibility for the deeds, was taken care of by God. Erased. Tossed as far as the East is from the West, to be remembered no more. So are we free to be as evil as we want with no consequences? See the previous chapter, 'The Big Miss,' for this discussion.

Scene 20

Laws to Protect Your Ass (well, your donkey, that is)

D: Could you expand on your discussion of the need for judgment and rules a bit further? Maybe discuss how all that works by explaining the role and reasons why God instituted the Mosaic law to the DOI in the first place. I mean, is the Law a bad thing? Or was it a good thing when God instituted it?

S: Well, first Paul definitely upholds the goodness of the Law of Moses (Romans 3:31; 7:7; 7:12, 7:14; 7:22) just as David also celebrates it with Psalm 119. The Law is a mirror reflection of God's character, and in that way, it is most excellent.

However, we know the Mosaic Law is not for Christian believers today (Romans 6:14, 7:6, 10:4, Colossians 2:14)—nor was it ever intended for anyone who wasn't one of the DOI[1]. But it can still be very valuable as an object lesson to all people.

From the last chapter, we see that 'judging'—in the sense of preventing people from hurting each other and the existence of consequences if and when they do—is not unloving, but actually the loving thing to do.

In light of this, laws are instituted in society so everyone knows what the boundaries are. That is only fair. However, the whole Mosaic Law thing gets a bad rap. Mostly from outside the church community, but also from the inside.

We think all those crazy laws in the Old Testament are a downer. Coveting, and all that crap.

We think—So what? The Ten Commandments? Who needs it? What does it mean anyway? Or better still, what did it mean to the people God gave it to?

The 613 Mosaic laws are mainly about protecting other people from you, and at other times it's about facilitating a fairness and rightness for you as an individual vis-à-vis everyone around you.

This means at its core, the spirit (or true meaning) of the Law was not about God judging and God being a mean, fun-busting ogre, but was actually about God's love.

God loved you enough to make other people well aware that if they did anything bad to you, they would have the power of God to reckon with. That was how much protection you had from other people's wrong-doing. But other people had that same protection against you.

Even more than this, and more shockingly to our modern minds, God actually instituted the Law to protect the DOI from destroying themselves in moral degeneration as they lived in the Promised Land. This was because of how good God was going to make it for them.

God said to his people through Moses in Deuteronomy 8, "It's going to be so good for you in the Promised Land—I'm going to give you so much, and do so much for you—that if you don't remember me and follow the rules I give you, you will end up destroying yourselves with how good you have it."(*my paraphrase*)

/thē·*il*·logical/ - 195

So again, the Mosaic Law, as God originally intended when he instituted it, was far from being the nasty, fun-busting, tyrannical shackler we think of today.

It was actually the opposite.

It was to insure that the good times for the Descendants of Isaac continued.

However, God's later opinion of the Law was that it sucked in its inadequacy to accomplish his ultimate goal, which was the closest, most intimate relationship he could possibly have with humans (Romans 7:10, Hebrews 7:11-28-especially vs. 18-19).

In the New Testament, Paul clearly tells us that living under these laws didn't work, because instead of people loving God more and more through the progression of the Old Testament, they actually hated him more and more as the law drove them further from God (Romans 7:5,10).

And we see that God's warning in Deuteronomy for those in the Promised Land proved right—God did give them everything, and they did get spoiled and forgot about him. They did become fat and proud and lazy on their riches and morally degenerated to the point of destroying themselves. They victimized each other and the nations around them to horrible degrees. They were well on their way to being Sodom and Gomorrah (Isaiah 1:9-10, Jeremiah 5-6; 7:21-26), or worse, when God stepped in and scattered them during the periods of exile.

We can see how the experiment of the Mosaic Law turned out. It was a complete disaster from start to finish. For humans, and for God. But it had purpose in that it showed that laws, rule-keeping and ritual do not result in people getting closer to God (his goal), but in fact, laws, rules and rituals have the exact opposite effect. They result in death and people being pushed further away from God.

Pretty much the only thing the Law accomplished was to show how separate and different we are as humans from God and his character. (And that's a very worthwhile thing to consider.)

So after a period of time where the DOI lived (and failed) under the Law, God sent his Son to live the Law perfectly, then die and rise from the dead in order to institute a brand new way of living (Hebrews 7: 18-19).

Through God's interaction with the DOI (*see appendix 1*), we see that Jesus killed off their 'marriage to the Law' so that God was now free to, in effect, marry his Spirit to all humans who want a friendship with God (Roman 7:1-6—especially verse 4, 2 Corinthians 5:20 MSG).

This is what it meant when Christ ushered in the kingdom of God.

D: Ok, so I'm thinking if Christ came to usher in the kingdom of God, he was in effect reinstituting the Garden of Eden, right?

S: Exactly. And now, since sin and death have been taken care of, God's main mission on earth is twofold: To destroy the rest of the enemies of God (not *human* enemies of God, but things like physical death—1 Corinthians 15:25-26), and to restore and heal creation (Romans 8:18-25).

D: If that's the case, why doesn't God instantly zap us out of this sinful and fallen world right away? Isn't it cruel for God to keep us in this messed up world? If he went through all that trouble with death on the cross to accomplish the sacrifice to free us, why not just bring the new heaven and new earth (Revelation 21-

22) *now*? What is he waiting for?

S: Time goes on and history continues because God desires everyone to come to him (1 Timothy 2:4) and those who presently live in God's kingdom on earth—the worldwide community of believers known as 'the church'—are an integral part of God's program, as they are 'his body,' God's literal presence on earth, as he actually resides in the community of believers, which are known now as the temple of God (replacing the physical temple in Jerusalem forever).

D: So why then are 'believers' or 'the church' often the worst representatives for God on earth, and usually doing things the opposite from what God wants? I mean, seriously—the church is so often doing harmful things instead of good.

S: Well, for one thing, as we mentioned before, God works through weak jars of clay.

In ourselves, we are still weak, physically limited beings, often subject to living in fear and worry and mistrust and disbelief that God will meet all our needs and take care of us fully. So we still do stupid and harmful things to ourselves and others in our commitment to look out for Number One.

The greatness of God is that in spite of that, God still gets his work done by loving the world through the community of believers.

For as much as the community of believers has done wrong, God has done a lot of things right through his people. Those who aren't his people have done a lot of things right too, maybe sometimes even more so when his people aren't paying attention to loving others.

It's amazing that in the Bible, we see God mainly chooses to work through extremely faulty and weak people. In fact, it seems he nearly always chooses to do things this way. Because in it, we see God. If someone like Gideon can take 300 people into battle against what scholars believe was an enemy force of hundreds of thousands—and win—then we know it had to be God (Judges 7:4-8; 7:12).

The more we rest (Matthew 11:28-30) and *not* choose to be involved in 'religion,' that is when God is at his most powerful (Matthew 5:3—MSG).

The history of the world has rarely, if ever, seen God and his love fully unrestrained through his people on earth.

Why?

Because we are always falling back into religion and not living in rest and freedom. The New Testament makes one thing perfectly clear: We can either live our lives in freedom, or in shackled slavery.[2]

Which do we want?

Which sounds better?

We're free to choose.[3]

---

[1] Galatians 4:4—Jesus was born under the Law because he was a descendent of Isaac. No reason for Paul to point this out if we are *all* born under the Law. He was born under the Law to redeem those under the Law, and through that, the whole world would be saved, first the Jews, then the Gentiles (Romans 1:16, 2:14, 3:2, 3:29, 9:30, Galatians 3:8, 3:14).

[2] Which includes, but is not limited to, all religion (including Christianity as a religion), secularism, materialism, agnosticism and atheism—any way of life apart from living in the freedom provided by the living, loving God.

[3] And even as believers sealed with the Spirit, we're *still* free to choose. Our eternal destiny is not in jeopardy, but day to day we can live in freedom with God, or in 'the flesh' (Galatians 5:16-18), under the tyranny of our limited physical selves.

Scene 21

I Will Choose...Free Will

D: I have another question about what it means to live in freedom.

S: Bring it.

D: Just to be clear about what you're saying: If everyone who's ever lived had their sins taken care of by Jesus 2,000 years ago, why wouldn't God force everyone to embrace his sacrifice knowing it's ultimately for their own good—like pulling a child from a busy street?

S: Good question. And I think the reason is because God respects our free will. We are not children, so God does not override our free will even when it's a slam dunk that it's for our best.

D: But who in their right mind *wouldn't* choose to live in perfect paradise?

S: Hmm...well, Adam and Eve, for starters. They didn't want to preserve paradise. They wanted to know what it was like to go their own way. Of course, they hardly knew what they were getting into, and what it would mean for the history of humanity when they made that decision. They thought they were choosing something better than what they had. It was a false promise, or lie, of the devil to them that if they turned *away* from God, things would be better.

God warned them not to do it. But he respected their free will.

Now we have the extreme benefit (crazy, I know, but I said it) of knowing exactly what going our own way from God looks like, and where it leads. And that *should* throw every one of us back into the arms of God faster than a cougar on the space shuttle—"Warp speed! Full ahead, Captain! Into the arms of God! I'M GIVIN' HER ALL I GOT!"

That is a slam dunk right there. And yet, many don't see it that way.

Adam and Eve lived in a perfect world in a perfect relationship with the loving God, the Master of the Universe standing right there beside them, and still they chose to reject him.

It shows that if a bunch of us had been in the Garden of Eden, instead of just two people, some of us would have stayed with God, but some still would have walked away. I totally believe that to be true.

We tend to give Adam and Eve a hard time. But we need to realize they were simply humans just like us. It's easy to demonize them and say, "I wouldn't have done that!" But is that really true? Of course there's no way of telling, all I'm saying is maybe we aren't as high and mighty above Adam and Eve as we might think.

After all, we have the benefit of seeing where things went. Adam and Eve did not. And it wasn't as if God didn't tell them what would happen. He did.

But wait—you say—he could have *shown* them.

Well, no he couldn't.

Because in the history of the universe, nothing like that had ever happened before. So even if he showed them, like John trying to describe events in Revelation, they wouldn't have understood it any more than John understood what he saw in Revelation. John doesn't tell us what Revelation means. He simply described what he saw, and that's what we're left with.

All of this boils down to 1 Corinthians 13: What love is—and conversely—what love is not.

Love does not force—love allows choice.

Do we want to come along with God? Or don't we?

We don't have to come.

God leaves it entirely up to us.

Isn't this the same as when we're interested in someone romantically?

Do we force?

Will that get the job done?

Or do we try to 'woo' them—make them dinner, or pay for a movie, be kind to them, and look out for their best interest over ours?

Isn't that how it's done?

And frustrating and painful as it can be when we are rejected, do we really want to change things and opt for the caveman style of smacking her over the head and dragging her back to our cave by her hair?

D: I've been single for a long time. That's starting to sound more tempting than it used to.

S: I hear you...but seriously...in answer to your overall question, the reason God doesn't 'beam us up' when we come to Christ is because from God's point of view, he's given us everything we need and promises to provide for all our needs and desires.

And yet, he's still using the fallen world, and our fallen selves, for purposes that are valuable to us and the world as a whole.

God shows his goodness and faithfulness, showing us himself, in the midst of our weakness, unfaithfulness, bad decisions and bad behavior.

That's why when James and John asked to be considered equal with Jesus in heaven, Jesus invited them to be tortured, whipped, spit on and abused, because that was what it took to reverse the effects of the fallen world (Matthew 20:22).

Needless to say, they didn't accept the invitation (Mark 14:50).

As people watch our lives, those who know us best will see God and experience God firsthand through our mere 'jars of clay' (Matthew 5:5—MSG).

Just as in the story of Gideon in Judges, when we see the impossible happen before our eyes, that is when we see God.

And really, could there be anything better than seeing God?

Paul says in Galatians 5 that when we live in 'the flesh,' we can block God's best from coming through.

Should we feel guilty about this?

No.

Because God is stronger and bigger than anything about us.

But according to Paul, it's best if we get ourselves out of the way in rest and let God 'do his thing.'

And we can see what the promise of living in rest gets us by looking at God's action with the physical Promised Land in Deuteronomy.

It is actually a picture of the original Garden of Eden economy.

> When the LORD your God brings you into the land he swore to your fathers, to Abraham, Isaac and Jacob, to give you—a land with large, flourishing cities you did not build, houses filled with all kinds of good things you did not provide, wells you did not dig, and vineyards and olive groves you did not plant... (Deuteronomy 6:10-11)

Later, in Deuteronomy 11:14-15, God tells them he will even control the weather so they will never go without crops and food.

In effect, I will do everything for you. You just do your work in non-stress and non-worry. Enjoy your earthly physical work knowing it will always be maximally fulfilling and rewarding.

But wait! There's more!

D: What? You're going to give me a set of Ginsu knives?

S: No. Better! The offer God gives us in Matthew 11:28-30 is even better than the one he gave the DOI in Deuteronomy.

D: How?

S: Because for the DOI, experiencing good things from God was contingent on them following and keeping his rules and laws, the Mosaic Law. But for us, Jesus did all the work. All the work is in the past.

Jesus said, "It is finished," so there is no contingency for us in order to experience good things from God. It's right there for us. We can run around like chickens with our heads cut off in activity, work and exhaustion for God...or we can rest, sit back and let him work everything out. And when we see him working things out, we can join in partnership with God in whatever is going on, just like entering the Promised Land. Just like when Peter waited until a show of the Holy Spirit before he got up to preach to the people at Pentecost. Jesus told him to wait for the Spirit to come, and he did.

Where was Peter when God asked him to go to Cornelius' house? Up on the roof praying, enjoying the afternoon and waiting for lunch.

When God gave the word, he got up and participated in what God was doing.

Until then, he waited. He rested in God.

God worked hard to set things up that way. So live in it. Enjoy it. Be free. Enjoy life.

Hebrews chapter 4 tells us the DOI never ever attained this 'rest.' Not even close. They could have, simply by believing God.[1] But they didn't. The Law always showed them to be failures.[2]

The prophets and people of God in the Old Testament had to live in anticipation of God coming and finishing things in the *future* (Hebrews 11:39-40).

But we live on the other side.

Where Jesus has finished things. Everything.

So now we can rest.

[1] But with contrite hearts before God, simply admitting they couldn't hold up to the Law, they could have experienced the same rest we can have today. And some of God's people in the Old Testament did live in God's rest, as they anticipated the coming Christ (Hebrews 11).

[2] Though the Bible makes it clear the Law is good (Romans 7:7,12,14). It shows us the character of the perfect God, which is to always take care of those around you. Completely outward focused. The opposite of selfishness. Jesus said the spirit of the Law is to 'Love others in the same way you love yourself.' That is the Law summed up, if you will. But it wasn't useful in doing what it was supposed to accomplish, which was to bring us back into the close, intimate relationship humans had with God in the Garden of Eden. And that is always where God wanted things to go. Now we can trust that he knows best, and always always always acts in our best interest. He proved that he has our best interest in mind by coming to earth (Philippians 2).

Scene 22

I Took a Guilt-Trip and Forgot To Pack My Underwear

S: Let me possibly be the first person in history to make this statement: There is no value for Christians in focusing on the torture of Christ.

D: *What?*

S: Hear me out:

Wouldn't it be weird if a few times a year I called up my father to chit-chat, pass news of our lives to each other and whatnot, and he always started out by saying, "Ok, before we talk, I want to remind you again how much I went through to put food in your mouth and shelter over your head when you were growing up. Let me tell you again about all the awful times I had, and how much I had to work and sacrifice to do it. It was awful, but I got you there."

Maybe some parents do lay this kind of guilt trip on their kids in subtle or not so subtle ways. But let's not call it anything other than what it is—a guilt-trip. And in my opinion, loving parents would never do that to their child, and neither would a loving God.

There's no value to Christians for God to guilt-trip us like that. And the great news is: He doesn't.

Guilt-tripping from God is not needed as a motivation

for us in our Christian lives. If we take Galatians 2:20 at face value, why would Christ need to guilt-trip himself in order to motivate himself to do something, or to obey God? It doesn't make sense. Again, Christ (God) lives his life through us. "It is no longer I who live," Paul said, "but Christ lives in me."

When I was a child, I doubt my father ever wanted me to know the full extent of how hard he had to work to put food in my mouth. I'm pretty sure he happily focused on the end result of his work—that his kids were happy, healthy, able to go to school and eventually have families of their own.

My father never once sat me down as an adult, or a child, and said, "Ok, let's remember what it took for me to give you what I gave you. First, I had to get up at 5:30am each day after a night of you crawling into my bed and kicking me all night...."

But what if my dad did start our conversation like that?

How would the rest of it go from there?

I might grovel a bit. I would certainly feel like crap, ashamed of what I made my dad go through. I wouldn't want to tell him any good news about my life, or even speak to him at all, because I'd feel so badly about myself.

Thankfully, I've never heard this kind of conversation from my dad, and I'm pretty sure I never will.

Why?

Because my dad loves me. He has never brought it up once.[1]

So why do we think God would want to?

Again, my dad made those sacrifices because he loved me. Not so he could rub it in my face for the rest of my life.

As far as he's concerned it's in the past, forgotten—never to be brought up again. And I don't think God, as our loving father, would want that kind of relationship either.

Now as far as the Lord's Supper is concerned, Paul does ask that Christ's sacrifice be remembered. Paul was asking that the result of the act be remembered, and be remembered in a celebratory way, not the guilt-tripping way most 'celebrate' the Lord's Supper (1 Corinthians 15 and 1 Corinthians 11).

D: But can't we get an understanding of the seriousness of sin from learning about the crucifixion, and from things like watching Mel Gibson's *The Passion of the Christ?* Isn't there value in that?

S: In a word: No.

Not that it wasn't a good and well-done movie. It was.

But since we already live in freedom-land (Romans 6), where would feeling massive guilt move us to? What use would it be?

For those of us who are free, there is no value in dredging up the past suffering and hardship that got us to that freedom.

However, there is still value in it for those who haven't yet embraced Christ.

It could be very valuable for someone to know what God went through for them, what it took for Jesus to be perfect on our behalf, what the love of God looks like in its truest, rawest form.

Also, the torture of Christ and the cross is a good picture of the seriousness of sin; the wrong doing we do against others—all the way from murder, racism, slavery, genocide, child molestation, rape, sex-trafficking, and third-world sweat-shops all the way down to bullying and office gossip. And God takes *all* of that very seriously.

In other words, our sin nature is so bad, it took nothing less than the torture and death of God himself to undo the mess.

I'd say that's pretty serious.

Consider this: Does God's love on the cross look like the picture of a monster that's against us? Does it look like the picture of someone who wants to shackle us under undue burdens of strict morality and never having fun? Does it look like the picture of someone who's looking for a certain standard of behavior from us, and if we fall short, he will turn his back on us? Does it look like the picture of someone who wants anything less than to give us the very best, our most valued and sought after desires, someone who wants to give us everything; the greatest, most fulfilled and exciting life we could possibly ever have, all the time, for all time?

That's the picture of God we get from the cross.

------

[1] As no analogy perfectly mirrors reality, this analogy breaks down in that, since my dad chose to have children, I'm not really ultimately culpable for kicking him at 2am and him having to get up at 5:30 to go to work. It was his choice to have me. So, yes, we do need to realize that the sin barrier that resides (resided) in us took a HUGE sacrifice for God to overcome, and the sin barrier is something WE are responsible for, not God. God made the world perfect and right, and humans rebelled. The value, once again, in even

mentioning the extent of the suffering for the accomplishment of Christ's sacrifice is for those who still have yet to embrace God's plan. They need to know there is a gulf between humans and God that is very serious. What God had to go through for them on the cross is something to really consider, but *not* as a guilt trip, but rather as a reality of the human situation. Again, you might say, 'well God chose for me to be born, so I am not responsible.' But again, that discounts the fact that even before you were born, God knew Christ would be sent as a solution. The ability to 'fall' had to be built into the framework of the world in order for free-will to exist, and for us not to be robots. Through a single choice, Adam plunged the world into chaos, but through a single choice Jesus fixed it (Romans 5). Free will is still in effect after Jesus, because God still seems to honor our choice to want to be with him or not. Otherwise, if Jesus' sacrifice took away all sin from all men for all time, then what is the value in continuing to have all of humanity living under the fallen nature of the universe? None that I can see. The only thing that makes sense is that God is still honoring his original free will agreement he's always had with humans. Do you want to be with me? If not, you're free to be on your own. Again, again, again, there is no value in God creating robots. Love is not love without risk and the choice to not love back; or rejection. Do you want to marry a robot, thus securing that you'd never ever have to suffer getting divorced? Maybe some of us would on a bad day. But at the end of our lives, that would have a million times less value to us than a partner who went through all the hard times with us, but CHOSE to stay with us. The value of them staying is rooted in the reality that they could have left. That has infinitely more value than a robot. But for us who have already embraced God's plan, I really doubt there is any value at all in dredging it up every chance we get, if ever at all.

212 - /thē·*il*·logical/

-Episode Three-

Freedom in Practice: James

Breakin' The Chains

Scene 23

James and the Giant Misinterpretation

D: I now have a new respect for Paul. He wasn't only writing about freedom, he was fully living it.

S: Absolutely. And his letter to the Galatians was his War Cry. The cool thing is that every book of the New Testament is livable. And that brings us to the book of James.

D: I'd always thought James' seemingly harsh behavioral edicts were difficult to live. This book has often heaped a ton of guilt on me, then I'd feel guilty for feeling guilty.

S: But that's not freedom. It's actually the opposite. Guilt is shackling, not freeing. Right?

D: Yes, I can see that. Viewing everything from the lens of freedom seems key.

S: So we see that far from being a disjointed book about rules and behaviors, James actually had one thought in mind when writing this book: What it means to live in freedom.

Just as Paul and the other New Testament writers wrote their letters in response to issues and questions they were dealing with in the early churches, so James' audience also had their own rocky road to travel while trying to figure out what freedom meant in practice.

The first thing we notice about the book of James is the genius of its organization. The brilliance of James jumps out at us in how the letter is arranged: Very tidy, very easy to follow, very easy to understand. Which means James might have been 'anal retentive.' And I don't mean that in a bad way, I mean it in a good way.

It also means James would've been a good lawyer—and again, I mean that in a good way.

James' audience is the communities of believers (churches) in and around Palestine shortly after Christ's death and ascension, largely made up of Jewish converts.

You've seen *Law and Order* on TV right?

D: I used to love that show. Seen it about a hundred times.

S: Good.

D:...maybe a hundred and five...

S: It's ok. Don't hurt yourself. But you know how the district attorney gives an opening statement before the jury? He talks about the case in summation form before launching into the evidence and making his broader case.

D: Yeah, he says stuff like: 'The evidence will show that the defendant stole a thousand dollars out of the victim's mattress, etc, etc.

S: Exactly. The evidence will 'show.' But he doesn't get right into it in the opening statement, right? Because this isn't the time in the trial for expanding on the evidence. That's for later.

D: Sure, I get that.

S: So if you hang onto that thought, then the book of James will make a lot more sense. Because that's exactly what James does in Chapter 1.

Instead of the book of James being a seeming hodgepodge of stand-alone statements about behavior and how to live the Christian life wisely, it's actually a well-organized argument for one overall point—the same point made in every other book of the New Testament—and that is: Live in your freedom. Do not make Jesus a religion. Protect that freedom. Do not let anyone or anything take your freedom from you.

James was addressing a community of believers spread throughout Palestine who were facing a severe persecution with far-reaching consequences in their everyday lives. But James pleads with them not to throw away the freedom that Christ lived and died to bring them.

He urges them in love to withstand the persecution—to take one for the team, so to speak—to not crumble under the pressure and go back to religion. He's emphasizing what Paul said in Galatians 5:1: "It is for freedom that Christ has set us free. *Stand firm, then, and do not let yourselves be burdened again by a yoke of slavery.*"

D: Makes sense so far. Can't wait to hear the rest.

S: James starts the book by encouraging the community of believers to *endure* hard circumstances, because these circumstances have *value*. They are not random or out of control useless 'happenings.' He urges them to pray specifically for guidance from God's spirit in this difficult time (James 1:5).

Then in James 1:9, he sets up a rich/poverty contrast to be expounded on later. Remember our lawyerly opening-statement analogy? He's not making a

/thē·il·logical/ - 217

general, universal statement about being rich or poor. He's showing solidarity with a group of poor people in these communities who were being treated in a way that diminished their dignity, and at the same time indicting a specific group of rich folks in these communities who James later reveals to be extremely corrupt. So with these verses, he's referring to s*pecific* groups of people at that time in those communities.

D: Ok, I'm with you. Keep going.

S: In James 1:13-18, he urges them to hold fast to the truth they know—he urges them to hold fast to their freedom in Christ.

Christ + Nothing.

> When tempted, no one should say, "God is tempting me." For God cannot be tempted by evil, nor does he tempt anyone; but each one is tempted when, by his own evil desire, he is dragged away and enticed. Then after desire has conceived, it gives birth to sin; and sin, when it is full-grown, gives birth to death. (James 1:13-18)

James exhorts them to avoid the temptation of falling back into 'religion,' or bowing to the 'temptation' of thinking the plan of 'Christ + Nothing' does not come from God. False teachers were making the argument that God himself wanted them to fall back into religion, or Christ + rules/rituals (in this case, to fall back into following part, or all, of the Mosaic Law).

To counter the argument of the false teachers, James tells them in vs. 16-17 that only *good things* come from God, and that since falling back into religion is *not* a good thing, therefore, it is obviously not from God. So don't abandon the plan of Christ + Nothing.

D: I always thought those verses were about temptations to sin that we face in our everyday lives today.

S: Yes, the part about 'being enticed by evil desires' is often interpreted to mean what we think of as 'acts of sin,' or bad behaviors. But this is far from James' intention. When he talks about being swept away with 'sin that leads to death,' the 'evil' and 'sin' he refers to is the abandonment of the freedom Christ lived and died to bring us. He urges us not to abandon Christ + Nothing by no longer trusting and believing that this is God's true and good plan.

To James, not living in freedom is equated with evil and sin.

His statement, "when sin is full-grown it gives birth to death" can be paralleled with Hebrews 6 and 10 in that if we decide to abandon our freedom and fall back into rule-keeping, laws and religion, we effectively cut ourselves off from the life of God. Living water can no longer flow as God wants it to. The bread of life becomes stale. We no longer have the opportunity to experience life and life abundantly. Instead we're choked off from God's power, the life of his spirit. And what we're left with is the opposite of life. We're left with death.

James warns against falling back into 'religion' in love for his audience. Because he wanted people to experience the full greatness of God; for them to have the best, most exciting, most fulfilling lives they possibly can, just as God intended for them.

D: That sounds better than being afraid my sin leads to death.

S: Yeah, see how that doesn't even make sense? Jesus said if you believe in him, you've crossed over from death to life. How could any kind of temptation and sin take that away?

D: That's right—I never thought about it that way.

S: James isn't going to say something contrary to Jesus, we know that much for sure. You ready for the next part of the opening statement now?

D: Bring it.

S: In James 1:19, James tells them that when you meet with each other as a community of believers, listen more than you speak. Be slow to get angry. And most importantly, don't be quick to speak (to use your tongue), but listen to the mature believers who teach the truth, not the lies of the false teachers. And further, if you are a relatively 'new' believer, then be quiet lest you repeat and spread the lies of the false teachers in your ignorance, thus, in effect, making you a false teacher as well.

So listen, and don't be quick to speak, because it can be monumentally damaging.

Again, this is a summary statement James will expound upon later in the book.

Then we come to James 1:22-25—the famous 'faith and deeds' discussion encapsulated (to also be expounded upon later in James' book):

> Do not merely listen to the word, and so deceive yourselves. Do what it says. Anyone who listens to the word but does not do what it says is like a man who looks at his face in the mirror and, after looking at himself, goes away and immediately forgets what he looks like. But the man who looks intently into the perfect law *that gives freedom,* and continues to do this, not forgetting what he has heard, but doing it—he will be blessed in what he does. (James 1:22-25, *italics mine*)

James tells them do what the truth telling teachers are

teaching you (the Word). Do live what you know is true about God and his plan. Do have faith (trust) that Jesus' work on the cross was sufficient for salvation, and to meet all your needs for your entire lives with God (Galatians 2:20, Galatians 3). And the fact that you believe this, and trust in it, is shown by your actions. And the action he's looking for is living in freedom and not falling back into religion, or adding anything to Christ's finished work.

They show they believe God's plan by the *action* of living in freedom from rule-keeping, laws, and religion and anything having to do with self-effort.

That is the *deed* that naturally follows from their faith.

And this action, this deed, has the added benefit of showing the persecutors that the believers in the church will actively *not* add anything (works, rules, rituals) to God's plan, thinking or believing that those extra things are needed for salvation, or for our everyday lives with God.

So to sum up, the deed that showed their trust in God was to not fall back into religion. To not bow to the pressure of the persecutors to add anything to the finished work of Christ, and especially to not fall back into trying to follow any of the Mosaic Law and its rituals.

Because none of these things are needed.

Christ said, "It is *finished*."

James urges them to trust God—to take God at his word—that the plan of Christ, the cross of Christ, is sufficient for everything.

Continuing in James 1:26-27, James tells them that practicing and/or falling back into religion (in their specific case, the Mosaic Law) only leads to hypocrisy, illogic and inconsistency in life.

Every time.

D: That does seem to be a major theme in the New Testament.

S: Yes. It's something we ought to pay attention to.

D: No doubt.

S: Ok, so now that James has addressed all these issues in summary statement form, let's get started as he makes his case to back up these summations, starting in James 2.

Scene 24

Show Me Yours, I'll Show You Mine

S: We talked about James making summary statements in chapter 1 just as a lawyer would make an opening statement before presenting his case. With that in mind, we see that James 1:12 and James 2:1 are sister verses:

> James 1: 12 states: "Anyone who meets a testing challenge head-on and manages to stick it out is mighty fortunate. For such persons loyally in love with God, the reward is *life and more life*." (MSG, *italics mine*)

> James 2:1 states: "My dear friends, don't let public opinion influence how you live out our glorious, Christ-oriented faith." (MSG)

So James 2 is going to unlock two pressing questions: *What* is the pressure causing the 'head-on challenge'? And *who* is instigating it?

From James 1:9 and 10, we learn that there was a contingent of financially wealthy religious people (DOI) visiting one or more of these believing communities[1] who were pressuring the church leaders[2] to have folks revert from living in freedom to go back to part, or all, of the Mosaic Law.

So what follows is a discussion where James, in effect, says, "Ok, you want to bow to that pressure? Can't endure it any longer, you say? You want to 'give in' and go back to living under law? Well, then, just as Jesus always said, 'if you want to live by the law, then you must keep the whole law, perfectly.'

The people in this church or churches tried to justify their buckling, accommodating actions by telling James, "Look, we're following 'love your neighbor as yourself'—isn't that a good thing? We're serving and honoring people in our church."

But James sees through it.

Yes, he responds, that's true. But you have conveniently chosen to serve and honor the rich and powerful, while ignoring the less financially and politically well-off among you. In others words, yes, you are keeping one law, but by the way you're doing it, you're violating another law. You're diminishing the dignity of an entire group of people in your community with this show of favoritism. And breaking one part of the Law of Moses is the same as breaking the whole Law.

So where are you now? James asks them. Where did that excuse get you?

By exposing all of this, James reveals this principle: This is exactly the reason why we don't live by the Law. Any of it. This is exactly why God tells us the Law is inadequate to get the job done, and why it doesn't work as a way to live.

James is telling them, if you try to live the Christian life by rule-keeping and law (instead of the spirit of God), you are functionally unable to do the right thing. Jesus showed this very clearly in the gospels. Paul also worked very hard in his letters to show that the Law is not adequate or able to bring everything together for the good and love of the whole community. Only Christ + Nothing in the power of God's spirit is able to do this.

Further, an insidious side-effect of living by rules and laws is that we manipulate them, picking and choosing what we like and don't like, to suit our purposes and our goals in exactly the way the leaders of these early communities of believers were doing.

Thus, James tells them, for all these reasons, falling back into religion is an illogical thing to do. A better way to live is to "speak and act as those who are going to be judged by the law that gives freedom" (James 2:12).

Then he gives an argument from logic by saying in James 2:14-17, what good does it do to claim you're living by the law that gives freedom (faith in Christ + Nothing), if you're not going to act on it, or live it?

But to cover themselves, some leaders came back to James in the first part of James 2:18 with, well ok, you and some in the church can follow God by the Spirit (the law that gives freedom; faith), but we are going to live our Christian lives by what we do, by following the Law (deeds).[3]

And James rightly attempts to re-unify the church by telling them this truth in the second part of 2:18: The two, faith and deeds, cannot be separated. They are like a married couple: They're one. Intertwined. Inseparable. Just like God's justice and God's love. They're not two separate concepts, but one.

To James, faith and deeds are inseparable; they're the same thing. He says in 2:20 (MSG), "Do you suppose for a minute that you can cut faith and works in half and not end up with a corpse?" The NIV reads, "Faith without deeds is useless."

James is telling them that living under the Law (deeds

without faith) will not produce what God wants. He showed them this earlier with the favoritism issue.

What will produce the good things God wants, and ultimately what we want, James argues, is embracing—getting on board with—God's plan for how it is to be done.

And James admits there is inherent risk in this.

He gives them an analogy from the life of Abraham which shows that faith, by its nature, is a deed, and it involves risk. A choice must be made (faith) and consequences result (deed) one way or the other.

God told Abraham the plan: "Sacrifice your son to me."[4]

I think it goes without saying that to embrace this plan, Abraham had to take a risk. He had to make a choice with consequences one way or the other. I'm sure he wondered, "God is asking me to kill my son. Is this going to end my son's life? Sure seems like it will. Will I lose my son forever then? Probably. However, God said he would make a great nation of me, with more descendants than sand on the seashore. So if I kill my son, how would he follow through on that promise? It makes no sense. Huh."

But ultimately, in Abraham's mind, with a backlog of experiencing the goodness of God's character throughout his life so far, he was able to trump any doubts and fears by reasoning, "Well, even if my son dies, God is able to bring him back from the dead, if he wants" (Hebrews 11:19).

And so he embraced—he agreed with—God's plan. He believed the plan, and acted accordingly.

Now if he merely said he believed the plan, but

continued sitting in his tent playing video games with Isaac, then he obviously never believed it to begin with.

But Abraham took the risk of embracing God's plan, trusting that if he killed his son, God could bring him back from the dead if he wanted to. And though he had an enormous backlog of experience with God, he still had to take a risk. Maybe this would be the one time God would not come through? Maybe this would be the time God would let him down?

He didn't know for sure. So it was a risk.

But the moment Abraham moved *one* muscle in his heart in the direction of God's plan (in other words: he had faith), James says, "That made him right with God" (James 2:23).

Salvation in an instant.[5]

This has always been the way of salvation for everyone, and always will be. By faith.

It would've made no sense for Abraham to say "Yes, God, I understand the plan. I believe it," but stayed home with Isaac to play X-Box. Then we, and God, and James, would rightly say he didn't really believe it.

So what about the audience of James' letter? What was James telling them about faith and deeds? And more importantly, what does this mean for us today?

James says God has clearly given us the plan: The cross has set us free from religion. So if you continue to strive to live the Law of Moses as if you were still under the Law (or, today, if we create new *mandatory* laws for the 'Christian' life--bible time, prayer time, quiet time, service to others, accountability groups-- that essentially *replace* the Law of Moses), then their, and our, faith is useless; dead. Their continuing to strive in the Law showed they did not believe (have faith in) God's plan, which would be the same as Abraham staying in his tent playing X-Box. In other words, if they continue to live the Law as if it were still a mandatory requirement between them and God, it shows they didn't, or haven't, really believed God's plan.[6]

James says living in freedom (the law that gives freedom) is the natural outworking of having faith that Jesus finished everything on the cross.

D: So I have a question.

S: Go ahead.

D: Is James telling them that if they follow the Law, they are in danger of Hell, and God's judgment? And if we ever add rules and rituals to Christ's finished work by making Christ a religion today, are we 'out' in God's eyes? In other words, do we need to stay on task with not adding anything to Christ's finished work, and if we don't, God is displeased? And further, are you saying that there is a plan that God individually gives to each of us (like in Abraham's case) that we must agree to and follow, and if not, we're 'out'?

S: I thought you said you had a question. Ha ha. In answer to that last part—No. Because for believers, the plan never changes. The plan was given clearly to all humanity 2,000 years ago. Abraham lived before Christ. We live after Christ (Hebrews 11:39-40).

The New Testament is very clear about this.

At the moment we have faith in God's plan, we are sealed with the spirit of God for all time (Ephesians 1:13-14).

Like Abraham, in that moment, you are made right with God.

So the deed, the 'muscle' that James' audience moves that shows they believe God's plan, is to never add anything to the finished work of Christ.[7] To never fall back into religion, especially back into trying to follow the Mosaic Law.

And for us today, same deal: Our deed as it pertains to believing in the finished work of Christ is not thinking religion, or anything else, is needed as an addition to the finished work of Christ.

I'd like to point out that we are 'saved' in a minute. In a second even. Just as Abraham was. And nothing will ever change that, or take it away, even if later we fall back into religion, or godless naturalism, or become a mass-murderer—or worse—a gossip! Once we are God's child, we are sealed with his Holy Spirit, and nothing will ever ever ever separate us from him. Ever (Romans 8:38-39).

D: Ever?

S: Ever.

Everything was taken care of the moment Jesus rose from the dead.

Every thing.

So God, Paul, James, and all of the New Testament writers implore us, for the sake of an abundant, exciting life, to understand our new identity. To be in partnership with God in what he is doing in the world. It's exciting. And you are free as believers and sealed children of God to come along.

Or not.

/thē·il·logical/ - 229

If you choose to have faith that Christ made you free but you never want to participate in God's plans, then there are no negative consequence from God for that. God is still, and always will be, for you and with you (Romans 8:38-39). Your eternal destiny is fixed. Heaven and Hell are not in question. You're sealed with the Holy Spirit, a joint heir with Christ.

God is always for you and with you. Always. Forever and ever (Hebrews 4:6-11).

D: And ever?

S: Hey, I keep saying it on purpose, because we're quick to forget this.

D: You're right. I'll stop harassing you.

S: Thank you.

Because it gets better than this, if that's even possible:

We see that the New Testament economy is about partnering with God's spirit to enact God's plans for the world.

We normally think: "Yeah, I like doing this God thing. I like doing this in my power and energy, along with God's power and energy (but only when direly needed), and together we make a pretty good team."

This is how most of our theology became a mix of law (our efforts) and the Spirit (God's efforts).

But the New Testament authors are clear that the way it works is that we piggy-back on God's spirit to do God's work.

We're simply along for the ride.

God invites us along. He wants us to be a part of what

he's doing.

So we see that God is better than we think, better than we ever thought he could be.[8]

And in light of this, James begs us, as Paul repeatedly did: Don't waste your time. Follow God and his plan now. Take him up on his plan. You won't regret it.

D: Wow, I really like what you're saying. But I need to call a 'time-out' for a second. I was wondering if you'd go back and expound on the whole 'risk' thing a little more. I'm still fuzzy on that. What was the risk they were facing?

S: In our day, we might consider all this and say, "Ok, James, I get it. It's pretty simple to place my faith in Christ and live it. What's the big deal?"

But we need to realize that today in the West we have freedom of religion, and for the most part folks are left alone to believe, or not believe, whatever they want.

But for the early church, this Jesus thing was a huge risk. All their lives these people had been told they had to follow massive amounts of rules and rituals (the Mosaic Law) to 'please' God. And now, all of a sudden, someone comes along and says, "No, it's not that. Actually God's plan is this: Christ + Nothing. No rules and rituals are needed. Ever."

That should rightly have caused a moment of pause.

A moment of great pause.

Frankly, it should've scared the crap out of them.

Because they might've thought, "What if I die and find out it really was all about following rules and rituals like the centuries of my ancestral history has been teaching us? Then I'm sunk! I'll probably go to Hell!"

James was well aware of this, and so was God, so he made sure to lovingly reassure them by saying, "Don't worry, I know it's a huge risk, but I'm telling you, it's the right plan. Trust me, trust it (the plan), and you'll be ok. But don't add anything to it. It's sufficient for the job. It's entirely sufficient to get you where you want to go."

Later, we'll see in Chapter 5, not only did James reassure them with words, but God was going to lovingly and supernaturally confirm to them that they could trust in what James was saying. God was going to give them a 'sign' as it were.

But more about that in chapter 5. I promise.

For us today, though, we might ask ourselves, "Do we really have it so much easier than James' crowd? Is there really little or no risk to believing in God's plan of Christ + Nothing?"

Ask yourself this: What competes for our faith today? What pressures do we face in believing God?

I can think of a million of them.

The fact that the Western world has largely thrown out the intellectual possibility that a 'supernatural' world exists. The notion that humans are simply bags of chemicals that eventually die and turn to dust, with no 'afterlife.' That believing in ourselves is best, that we can make things happen, we can make our lives work if we try hard enough, if we just want it bad enough (as taught in the popular book, *The Secret*). That the material world is all there is, and there's nothing more.

If we are to 'risk' thinking and believing that God does exist, we will find ourselves living very different lives than many others around us. Our friends, our family, the greater culture we live in might think and believe that their limited finite selves, and the limited finite resources that they can see on earth around them is all that exists. And they live accordingly, which is very different from believing and/or knowing that the God of infinite resources promises to always take care of us, for all time, in any and all circumstances, for our best interest. Always. Period. (Again, this is not 'health and wealth gospel.' What we think is in our best interest and what God thinks is in our best interest can sometimes, or often, be at odds (Isaiah 55:8-9). But can he be trusted? That is the question continually before us. But our ability to trust him in greater and greater ways, for greater and greater things and needs, is what it means to mature as a believer.)

So back to our discussion, we see today there is enormous pressure on us as believers. Because every day, by the way we live contrasted with others, we are forced to ask ourselves in the exact same way James' crowd had to ask themselves: "*What if we're wrong?*"

What if God is not there? What if another 'belief system' (world religion) is true, and Jesus doesn't exist at all? What if *The Secret* really is the key to life?

If so, we're missing out.

And that could spell huge trouble for us.

Paul of Tarsus was no dummy. He said in 1 Corinthians 15:16-19:

> If corpses can't be raised, then Christ wasn't, because he was indeed dead. And if Christ wasn't raised, then all you're doing is wandering about in the dark, as lost as ever. It's even worse for those who died hoping in Christ and resurrection, because they're already in their graves. If all we get out of Christ is a little inspiration for a few short years, we're a pretty sorry lot. (1 Corinthians 15:16-19-

MSG)

So having faith involves just as much risk for us today as it did in James' day.

But we need, as James exhorts his audience, to keep going. To protect our freedom and not trade it away for *anything.* And we can rest assured that God—as we'll see him do in James chapter 5—has ways (sometimes in supernatural ways, but not always) to show us he is there, he is concerned, and he loves us.

Now I want to do a little review session for those who might want to go over this again. If you think you've got it, then stop here and take a break if you like—go take a walk in the woods or get a cup of hot, steaming delicious coffee—then come back and go on to the next chapter. Ok? We'll see you then.

For everyone else, here we go.

To review: For *us* today—what is *our* action that shows we 'believe' God's plan?

The same as for James' crowd.

That the cross was sufficient to take care of everything that is not right between us and God. There is no longer any need for any Law or religion, or anything, *required* from us vis-vis our relationship to God.

We live in freedom and eternity is secure. God is always with us and for us.

We are not to add works, or idols, or superstitions, or wrong impressions of God, judgments of ourselves or others, to the finished work of Christ—we are to add nothing, nothing, nothing to the simple message of freedom in Christ (Galatians 5:1).

We are to live each day in rest in our inner-spirits and

piggy-back on God's spirit (Galatians 2:20, Galatians Chapter 3 and 5) as we wait on God, and watch what he does in the world. And when appropriate, we join in what he's doing in *his* power and effort, not our own.

Paul says Christ has set you free, so now that you are free, live free!

Live in your identity as free persons; no longer living as slaves. It makes no sense to live as slaves now, because you are legally free (Romans 6-7:1-6).

Again, in Galatians 5, Paul tells us we still have the choice to meet our needs our own way, or we can let God do it.

Our choice.

And how do we let God do it? By a theme that runs thick throughout the whole Old Testament—we wait.

We wait on God.

But that is a whole other book.

For now, we are free from the shackles and burdens of striving to live morally in our own power apart from God. Nothing else is needed besides Christ and Christ alone for us to experience life to its most full abundance.[9]

So before I beat this dead horse until it bleeds all over my laptop, let's conclude this discussion by asking this question: What has been the ultimate outcome of James bringing forth this discussion of faith and deeds?

Answer: The fact that we don't walk down the street and see a sign on a church that reads: *Church of Jesus Christ Combined with Jewish Rules and Rituals.*

No, we don't see that.

We only see 'Church of Jesus Christ,' as it should be.

If not for New Testament books such as James' letter, it's highly likely that Jewish rules and rituals would have crept back in and taken over the early church, since we as humans love and crave 'religion.' Eventually, or even right away, Jesus would have been crowded out completely, and all we'd have left is empty, inadequate religion.

Now, sadly today, theology is at a point where we haven't so much added laws like "be sure to give your donkey a drink before you tie it up and leave it" as much as we've come up with more sophisticated ways to crowd out Jesus by mixing law and grace—by living in continual cycles of 'try to be good-sin-fail-go to the foot of the cross-repent-have a contrite heart-accept God's grace-go out and give it another go' as we try to sanctify ourselves (supposedly in partnership with God) and strive toward the goal of becoming 'like Christ.' It's exhausting talking about it, much less trying to live that way.

We've made Christianity a religion.

And there's only one problem with that: Paul and all the New Testament writers told us never to live the Christian life like that.

---

[1] Either as believers or non-believers—this is not clear—and in either one or more or all the churches, equally not clear.

[2] Again, in one or more of the churches, probably several or most or all.

[3] Probably the latter group's motivation was that this allows them to suck-up to the group putting pressure on them,

thus relieving their persecution.

[4] People accuse God of being barbaric in asking Abraham to do this, but it was a foreshadow of Christ. God had it all under control. Point of fact: Abraham did *not* lose his son. But God did lose Jesus, for three days in death, and wonder of wonders, he raised from the dead. Nice foreshadow, God! Thanks for the hint, written into history more than a thousand years before Christ was born.

[5] Notice there is no mention of Abraham's sin problem, or the sin barrier between God and humans, or Abraham's 'sin' before God, in this *salvation* story.

[6] There are many disciplines that are good for us, but they are only for our personal benefit and the benefit of others around us. They don't affect our 'standing' with God. He has everything and he's fine. Quiet times, Bible study, contemplative prayers and meditations, service to others, accountability groups and any and all other valid Christian disciplines are important. But if they become a system to measure how we are 'doing' with God, or worse, how *we* measure how *others* are 'doing' with God, then we're missing the mark. Christian disciplines are healthy if we keep them in correct perspective—mostly the same way we discipline ourselves to get out of bed for work or to brush our teeth—because these actions are beneficial to our lives in one way or another. Not because teeth-brushing or alarm clocks determine my value or worth.

[7] The danger here isn't our eternal lives with God. No. Nor was this a danger for James' audience either. The "danger" in question is putting ourselves back under slavery; a non-free way of life. An unprofitable way of life. To us, and to those around us. Choking out our, and others', access to the spirit of the living God. This is what Hebrews 6 and 10 address. We are not in danger of cutting ourselves off from God or eternal life (Romans 8:38), but we are in danger of cutting ourselves off from living a free life in Christ and putting ourselves under slavery.

[8] Some of you might be asking, "But I like to work. I like to do God's work. What's wrong with that?" Nothing. We're not talking about not ever doing anything. We're not advocating

a passive Christianity. Far from it. Read the story of Peter and Cornelius in Acts 10 to see how we 'partner' with God. It's all done in God's initiation and power. Notice how Peter went along and participated in God's adventure.

[9] Now, of course, this question will come up: So what about when we might be in the position of leading a community of believers and we're looking around wondering: How do we know for sure any given person we see is 'right with God.' Fruit of the Spirit? Maybe, maybe not. I think the correct answer is this: We don't know for sure. God is the ultimate judge of our hearts, isn't he? We can't make this definitive assessment for those around us. We can come close maybe, but we're never the last word. God is. But what if you are a 'church' leader? Sometimes it's necessary to discern in love who seems to be 'with God' and who doesn't seem to be 'getting it'—perhaps, as Paul says in 1 Corinthians 15, so you can do some more persuading of them to be reconciled to God. After all, a church isn't just a club to hang out in. There's a lot going on among believers. There's a lot of discussion centering around how best to love the world through the power of the Spirit. And if you don't have the Spirit, and are never interested in doing so, then there probably comes a time when you might be prompted to find a club that better fits your needs and desires. So I will say this: Let's say a Buddhist comes to understand God's plan and says they believe it. But they still go and do all the rituals related to Buddhism on a regular basis. At some point, we might take them aside and ask, "Hey, it looks like maybe you don't really believe in God's plan." And they may say they are weak, or scared. This could be a legitimate response. And that is when we can immediately move right in there and lovingly help them out, as James did with his audience, and as the author of Hebrews did with that audience, etc. etc. Paul says to love and help the weaker (which may include scared—a weakness) believers among us. This is a good rule of thumb, agreed? But what if after a time, you and others have addressed their fears and weaknesses and are willing to support them 100% in the transition to embrace God's plan, and yet they still keep doing the rituals? Then we rebuke them, tell them to shape up, throw them out of 'the church' and never talk to them again, right? No. We have the freedom to let them continue to hang out in church as long as they want. Forever, if they

and we want to. But after an obvious amount of time goes by, we may, in our freedom as church leaders, also decide that maybe it's best that they should spend more time in their commitment to their Buddhist faith and its program, as we continue to be committed to ours.

Scene 25

Sit the *F Down, and Shut the *F Up

D: Wow, I need a break after that last chapter. That was deep. Good stuff.

S: Are you all right?

D: I'll be ok. Just give me a minute. Whew!

S: Take your time.

D: Ok, I've got my coffee. I'm ready to continue.

S: You sure?

D: Yeah, yeah. I'm sure.

S: Ok, we're moving on to James chapter 3. Got your Bible open and ready?

D: Got it.

S: Good. Strap on your helmet and hang on tight:

It's commonly thought that with this statement in James 3:1, "Not many of you should presume to be teachers" (TNIV), James is upholding the 'high office' of the pastorate.

But a closer look at this might reveal that he was speaking specifically to people in these communities of believers who were giving advice (teaching) about things of God that were inaccurate at best, and totally misleading at worst.

By making this statement, James was trying to cut-off the spread of partial or half-truths about God. "Be listeners," he tells these people in their specific situation.

By saying this, I'm thinking James is not teaching us as believers today a general principle of the benefits of being a 'good listener' as opposed to being someone who always talks too much, or always runs off at the mouth without thinking.

I think James is saying: Most of you are not telling others the truth accurately, so shut your mouths for a while, quit presuming to be a 'teacher,' be a listener for a while, and don't get angry about it—possibly referring to pride-busting quarrels about who should, and shouldn't, be teaching.

James continues in this context with a discussion of 'the tongue:'

> When we put bits into the mouths of horses to make them obey us, we can turn the whole animal. Or take ships as an example. Although they are so large and are driven by strong winds, they are steered by a very small rudder wherever the pilot wants to go. Likewise, the tongue is a small part of the body, but it makes great boasts. Consider what a great forest is set on fire by a small spark. The tongue also is a fire, a world of evil among the parts of the body. It corrupts the whole body, sets the whole course of one's life on fire, and is itself set on fire by hell. All kinds of animals, birds, reptiles and sea creatures are being tamed and have been tamed by mankind, but no human being can tame the tongue. It is a restless evil, full of deadly poison. With the tongue we praise our Lord and Father, and with it we curse human beings, who have been made in God's likeness. (James 3:3-9)

I'm thinking this passage was never intended to be a general principle on 'watching our mouths since our words can be harmful and painful.' This interpretation has possibly laid undo guilt on extroverts who have a tendency to speak before they think.

I believe James is merely saying, "Look, when you teach inaccuracies about God it can do a lot of damage. What is taught about God is powerful, and it needs to be accurate, because this is the place, *the only place*, where people can find—and receive—total freedom, total power, total rest from their burdens, totally abundant life; a totally satisfying and exciting existence.

So in light of that, if you're an immature believer, close your mouth for a while, and listen. Don't get angry, but take the opportunity to learn the accurate truth about God before you presume to be a 'teacher.' Because your words have the power to steer people into life, or steer them into death, down a dead-end, destructive road (in this case, adding 'religion'— traditional Mosaic rules and rituals—to Jesus, which chokes people off from the life of God).

James' point is backed up by the context that continues in James 3:10-12, where he comments on the mixing of false teaching with accurate teaching:

> Out of the same mouth come praise and cursing. My brothers and sisters, this should not be. Can both fresh water and salt water flow from the same spring? My brothers and sisters, can a fig tree bear olives, or a grapevine bear figs? Neither can a salt spring produce fresh water. (James 3:10-12)

James says on one occasion, accurate teaching about God is taught—and people discover the life of God. And another day, totally wrong and misleading information about God is taught, and people are choked off from God, which leads to death.

James is merely saying that the teaching within the community of believers should be consistent and accurate.

D: Beautiful words, man. I like it. Keep going.

S: Now in James 3:13-18 we see there was a boasting and arrogance problem in these communities that was divisive. People 'puffing themselves up.' And the result was un-love: a disunity, a divisiveness in mean-spirited competition. Instead of continuing down that road, James exhorts them to treat each other with dignity and honor. That is the way of God.

Which leads us to an unfortunate chapter break, because this same discussion goes all the way through James 4:12.

There was a deep-seated selfishness going on. A deep-seated commitment to 'wanting my own way.'

Then James, in 4:13, with scathing commentary, again indicts those who were the 'rich' in these communities:

> Now listen, you who say, "Today or tomorrow we will go to this or that city, spend a year there, carry on business and make money." Why, you do not even know what will happen tomorrow. What is your life? You are a mist that appears for a little while and then vanishes. Instead, you ought to say, "If it is the Lord's will, we will live and do this or that." As it is, you boast in your arrogant schemes. All such boasting is evil. If anyone, then, knows the good they ought to do and doesn't do it, it is sin for them. (James 4:13-17)

How do we know James was addressing the rich again

with these verses? Because he uses the same imagery here as when he addressed them in chapter 1 vs. 10. There he said that their lives could pass away in an insignificant moment, like a withering, wilting, wild flower.

Here, he says the same thing: You are a mist that appears for a little while and then vanishes.

He is emphasizing the temporal nature of their lives.

He is playing on the fact that the rich are those who (no matter what time period or culture you're in) are the ones people look up to; what we all aspire too; what we envy; lives we want for ourselves.

What they have is what we all want.

But James is wise. He knows, such as the Book of Ecclesiastes claims, that apart from God all is meaningless, a chasing after the wind. But *with* God, all is given proper context, and life has rich meaning and value.

Most significantly in these verses, however, is that James again shows solidarity with the 'poor;' the everyday normal believer in the community, by turning the tables on the rich persecutors.

As with the Pharisees in Jesus' day, those in power who followed the Mosaic Law tradition arrogantly saw themselves as 'righteous,' and everyone else, especially those who did not follow the Law, as 'sinners.'

James calls what they are doing, or more specifically, the attitude they are holding, to be sin.

He is calling *them* 'sinners.' Those who were most likely going around calling everyone *else* sinners.

James does this again brilliantly at the end of his

book, as he says about those who were 'wandering away from the truth' (those wandering away from freedom: aka Christ + Nothing, only to get mired again in the Mosaic Law), he says about them, "If anyone turns a *sinner* from the error of his way will save him from death and cover over a multitude of *sins*. (ch. 5:20)

Ouch. Wow.

That ought to rankle a few feathers in the power structure, to say the least.

And I'm sure James was hoping it did.

Scene 26

God: "I Got Yer Back"

S: Ok, moving on to Chapter 5: James continues to addresses the financially rich 'religious' who came into the community of believers and were given preferential treatment because the church was intimidated by them—after all, they had the power to be persecutors.

Being rich, they thought they deserved this preferential treatment. And as we see from chapter one, it was causing the church to bow to the pressure to accommodate them, taking things to such extremes that it forced the church to come up with hypocritical statements like, "We were just loving them as we love ourselves...," etc.

The community of believers had wedged themselves into a position where they could appease the potentially persecuting rich 'religious people,' and at the same time appease James' urging them to love each other.

And it created one big, hot mess.

In DOI society, wealth was a sign that you were 'in' with God. The contract of the Mosaic Law stipulated this. It was the original, and only, God-mandated health and wealth gospel the world has ever known: If you follow God's commands, you *would be blessed.*[1]

The problem is, as the New Testament writers labored continually to point out, after Jesus' resurrection, the

Law contract became void.

Not destroyed. But void.

This is because the new contract (a contract is actually a covenant) trumps the old contract completely and entirely (Romans 7:6). Not only that, but the new covenant is what God intended for humans all along, since the foundation of the world (Ephesians 1-3).

With this fact in mind—that Jesus' resurrection voided the Law contract in favor of a new covenant—James in 5:1-6 does what the church was afraid to do, what the community of believers was bullied away from doing.

James takes the bull by the nuts and exposes these guys.

He tells the churches, "You know what, these guys are not wealthy and in their privileged position because they are 'in,' or 'right' with God. No! In fact, just the opposite. They're actually oppressing and mistreating people in the worst form of social injustice. That is where their wealth is coming from. Not from God."

Harsh words, but true.

By exposing these guys, James is attempting to give the everyday church 'member' the strength to stand up and see these guys for who, and what, they really are: Religious charlatans and hypocrites.

He's telling them, in effect: "They don't even follow their own law that they are persecuting and pressuring you to follow!"

James, rightfully, has strong words for this situation.

But James is astute enough to know that these words will probably create a backlash of persecution in these churches[2], and even more so if the believers themselves decide to confront the phonies.

So in James 5:7-8, James lets them know they can stay the course; they can *endure* and take heart, because Jesus can 'show up at any time.' Jesus can relieve their suffering at any moment.

> Be patient, then, brothers and sisters, until the Lord's coming. See how the farmer waits for the land to yield its valuable crop, patiently waiting for the autumn and spring rains. You too, be patient and stand firm, because the Lord's coming is near. (James 5:7-8)

They can expect that Jesus will relieve their suffering in his timing, either by physically coming back to earth (as Peter looked forward to in his letters), or, more likely, by a relief program of encouragement from the outside, for example, by people like James who were aware of their situation.

God has infinite methods at his disposal to take care of his children and meet their needs, especially in situations where they're suffering for *him* and his cause (1 Peter 3:8-18). He can choose by supernatural means to look after them and relieve their suffering (such as the examples of early believers being let out of jail miraculously in Acts 12:6-11). Or he can do it through everyday people like James.

So James goes on encouraging them in this vein: He says, "Look, the prophets stayed the course in living lives for God in an evil and messed up world that persecuted them severely."

Then he brings up the example of one who arguably suffered more than any human in history—the original sufferer—Job.

James tells them, "Look, Job stayed the course, and in the end, it all came together for him. God honored, relieved and rewarded him. That is what you can look forward to with God. Guaranteed. So stick it out. Stick with the plan of Jesus + Nothing. It's the right course. God is with you, even when it looks like he's far away. He's not far away. He's right there with you, ready to relieve your suffering at any given second in his wisdom and timing. So take heart."

Then in James 5:12 he tells them in essence, "In this persecution and hard time, be honest. Call a spade a spade. Don't try to give the impression that by the things you do, or especially things you say, that you're going to 'persuade' God to do anything, good or bad, to change his timing about the current situation."

In other words, don't be superstitious.

It doesn't work that way.

So don't think that by changing your behavior, or by doing things like saying "in Jesus' name" at the end of a prayer instead of just "amen," or just leaving the end of a prayer hanging, that this is going to make God change anything.

Don't be superstitious like that.

I know it's hard, James is telling them, but just live life normally, trusting in God's timing, because nothing you do hurries up, or slows down, God's timing.

So relax, rest in God. Endure the suffering. He can and will relieve you at a moment's notice. He has that capability.

And the way God showed them he was with them was by doing what comes next.

S: Ok, time out. Remember when I told you a little bit ago that God was going to show them he was with them, and that they could take the risk and trust in what James was telling them?

D: Yes.

S: Well, here it comes:

God is going to confirm that he is with them by doing a 'miracle' in their midst. He was going to throw them a bone, as it were, to confirm that they can believe and trust what James was telling them.

In James 5:14, he asks them, "Is anyone sick? Have him go to the church leaders and lay hands on him and the Lord will raise him up."

James, being led by the Holy Spirit, somehow understands that God wants to heal someone in this community of believers, and that is how God is going to show these folks that He's behind them and that James is speaking the truth about God.

It's important to note this is a one-off healing, and we are not to take away any universal meaning here for us in our day because of it. Just as with the whole New Testament, yea, the whole Bible, the meaning for us in our day is the same thing it meant to the audience receiving it.

In the case of James 5, the meaning is that God does not ask us to take risks and then leave us high and dry.

He is not silent.

He does take care of us whenever we ask, and especially when he asks something of us.

We respond to his leading, and he shows he's right there alongside us, especially when and if suffering is involved.

What does this look like for us? Anything God wants it to look like. To James' audience it was the healing of a sick person, or persons, in their midst.

> Is anyone among you sick? Let them call the elders of the church to pray over them and anoint them with oil in the name of the Lord. And the prayer offered in faith will make the sick person well; the Lord will raise them up. If they have sinned, they will be forgiven. (James 5:14-15)

To us, it might be a healing, but most likely, something completely different. Because we have completely different lives in completely different contexts and circumstances than James' audience.

I think sometimes we take passages like James 5:14-15, where James says God will heal someone in their midst, to be a universal teaching applicable for all time. That James is saying to all Christians throughout history, "Pray for the physically infirmed, have faith that God will heal them, and God *will* heal them."

But I'm thinking this healing in James was a one-off event specific to the situation of that community of believers as God had in mind to communicate to them he was with them in their suffering and hadn't abandoned or forgotten them.

The message for us today is quite clear: When we risk ourselves, when we put ourselves at a disadvantage or suffer discomfort or persecution for the greater purposes of God, he will be with us. He has ways of showing he's with us and hasn't forgotten us in our suffering and pain.

But he can show us this in an infinite amount of ways, any way he likes, in fact. And not just through physical healings, something the church seems to get overly fixated on from time to time.

So what do you think? Are you ready to explore this idea of God and his miraculous power some more, and what it means to us today?

D: I'm ready.

---

[1] This is where the Christian 'health and wealth' gospel comes from. It results from thinking the Mosaic Law applies to us as believers today; that it's still a binding covenant or contract. The truth is, we live under a brand new, totally different covenant now, and as Gentiles, we never lived under the Mosaic Law to begin with. It was never binding to anyone other than the Descendants of Isaac.

[2] Which was his first point of the letter—to encourage them to endure under difficult circumstances. To not bail out early. To stay with Jesus + Nothing, and not run back to 'Egypt.' To not give in to the pressure to add DOI rules and rituals to what they are doing. To not see health and wealth as a sign of God's favor, but that actually the opposite is true, the privileged (in this case) are the unjust, the 'murderers.' The poor are God's people.

Scene 27

I Came Out of Gallbladder Surgery Missing My Left Leg

S: I've had a blurry right eye since birth.

D: I didn't know that.

S: It's true. My left eye is 20/20, but my right eye has never been in focus.

Sometime in my tweener years, a friend invited my brother and me to a church meeting with a guest faith-healer.

I went to the meeting, more skeptical than excited, but I went nonetheless.

Because who knew? What if I come away healed? I figured there was only upside.

When the faith-healer invited all who wanted to be healed to come forward, I fidgeted in my chair.

Having also been inflicted with extreme shyness where in most situations I'd rather die than draw attention to myself, I gathered all the courage I could muster, stood and went forward.

But not before snagging my brother's arm. "You're coming with me."

I went forward (brother in tow), waited my turn, and like Santa at the mall at Christmas, told the 'healer' about my aliment.

He asked me to close my right eye and rubbed a bit of olive oil on my eyelid, said a short prayer and asked me to open it.

"Better?" he asked.

I won't lie, I was really excited.

Was I really going to open my eye and see clearly?

For the first time ever?

Well, I opened my eye... and guess what?

I WAS HEALED!

No, just kidding.

I wasn't healed.

Holding a hand over my left eye, I nodded a sheepish "Yes" to the blurry-blobbish figure before me.

I lied.

But what else was I to do?

As the most bashful kid in the world, was I going to call this guy out on the carpet for the reckless sham that he was?

To this day, I am still embarrassed I got out of my chair, much less got my hopes up.

Luckily, it didn't shatter my faith in God, but I did go away wondering, *Why wouldn't God want to heal me?*

But let's look at the big picture of this incident for a

moment: As for the so-called faith-healer, he did nothing but embarrass himself and do damage to God's reputation before me and the entire church.

And that's something God doesn't take lightly.

In the Old Testament, false prophets were to be *killed*.

That's right.

If anyone claimed to speak for God, or claimed to act directly on God's behalf, and they were shown to be wrong, they were to be immediately put to death without mercy.

D: Wow, that's harsh!

S: But is it?

After all, do we really want the hard work of sifting through claims from every Tom, Dick, and Jane that something they tell us, or something they're doing, is directly from God?

I don't.

Much easier for me if they're simply incinerated.

Just kidding. What I mean is it's better for all of us, and for God's reputation, if everyone just keeps their mouth shut unless they're 100% sure they are speaking or acting for God.

That's as it should be.

And God didn't want the people of the DOI to waste their time with that either. It was the *right thing for him to do* to sift out the charlatans, and make clearly known that if you went there, there'd literally be Hell to pay.

He kept things simple. Very simple.

And I think it's great.

Unless you are absolutely 100% sure you are speaking for God, or acting on his direct orders, then please keep quiet and quit bothering me and the nice people.

As a human, I think if this warning and consequence to the DOI were still in effect today, it would greatly simplify things and I'd be all for it. But alas, like Jonah, I have to admit, "God, you are merciful. So much more merciful than I will ever be."

But now that God is merciful, it means we have to put up with the consequences.

Today we know exactly the effect of people going around 'speaking' for God with fake, hit-or-miss faith healings and other such chicanery. It has created a culture of extreme cynicism to the point where people think no one can, or ever has, spoken for God.

We should not, as believers, 'throw out fishing lines' and see what happens.

Because God is not hit or miss. He wasn't like that in the Old Testament, he isn't in the New Testament, and he's still not like that today.

God is exactly right and perfect, every single time.

Not long ago I was sitting in a coffee house with some believer friends when a woman I'd just met a few days prior interrupted the normal flow of conversation to look at me and say, "God is telling me right now that you are, or have been, somehow involved in architecture. I'm getting a word from God about you and architecture."

I looked at her and blinked a few times, wondering if

she was serious.

Sadly, she was.

I squirmed in my chair a few seconds, racked my brain for any signs of architecture in my past or present. And outside of watching way too much Brady Bunch as a kid (Mr. Brady was an architect), I could come up with nothing.

No-*thing*.

I didn't want to embarrass her, remembering the fake faith-healer of my youth, but I was an adult now and felt I had to tell the truth. "I've never been involved in architecture in any way in my life. Sorry."

She looked at me and said, in all seriousness, "Well, I'm new at this. I'm still practicing."

Practicing?

Practicing speaking on behalf of the God of the universe?

I just looked at her and thought, *No, no, no, honey. You don't get it. There is no practicing. In fact, you're damn lucky this isn't Old Testament times or we'd have to take you out back this here mall and kill you.*

As mentioned before, today we don't kill false prophets. God is merciful. Which is probably good, otherwise there might not be many people left on earth.

Today, we don't follow the Law and we aren't 'under the Law.' Nobody is under the Law as far as God is concerned.

We can voluntarily put ourselves under Law, but to God, that is foolishness. The Law had its day and was found by God to be insufficient. So he brought Christ into the picture. The fulfillment of the Law on our behalf.

Instead of the Law, today we operate under the principle of what is 'profitable' and what is 'unprofitable' (1 Corinthians 6:12; 10:23).

So I ask you: Is telling people that God will heal them through us, and then it doesn't happen, profitable?

I would have to say, no, it's not.

And not only that, it's still as damaging to God's reputation as it was in Old Testament times. And this applies not just in the realm of physical healing. Same thing applies to telling people, "I have a message from God for you," when we simply don't know if it's just coming from our own heads.

Again, when we are proven, or shown, to be *wrong*, we embarrass ourselves, everyone around us, and cause unnecessary confusion and embarrassment for God.

We make him seem unreliable, disreputable, and untrustworthy.

Is that the impression we want to give others of God?

Is that the impression God would want anyone to have of himself?

It's simply *unprofitable.*

I've been in some meetings lately with groups of believers where someone with serious hurts stands up and the group leader says, "We're now going to pray in the expectation that God heals you."

But when it doesn't happen (which has always been the case in my presence, so maybe I'm the problem?)

the whole event turns out to be patently un-loving.

The hurting person is let down—not built up. The hurting person is disappointed—not fulfilled. The person is left in confusion as to why God did not act, instead of being relieved of their pain.

This kind of stuff just makes people uncomfortable all the way around. And it's simply not love, so it'd be a tough sell to say it's of the Spirit.

Does that mean it never happens? That no one has ever been healed? Well, no. I believe it does, and has, happened.

But praying to God in the knowledge that God can heal, but not *expecting* him to, seems more Biblically sound. I don't see this as having a lack of faith, or lack of ultimate trust in God.

Do we really have the right to tell God what he is or isn't going to do? That's ludicrous. This thinking might be based on the idea, "Of course God wants people healed and healthy, so we are naming and claiming that desire of God..."

However, by doing this, you are still dictating to God what he should or shouldn't, will or won't, better or better not do. And God will never be boxed in and controlled by us in that way.

Of course God desires all people to be healed and healthy, however, he doesn't promise full, ultimate and complete healing for every believer in this lifetime.

Some believers are tortured in jail. Some are sawed in half. Some die of cancer. Some are killed in car wrecks and some will have chronic acne for the rest of their lives.

That's just how it is.

But that doesn't mean we can't ask God to remove it. Even Paul did this. But when God didn't fulfill Paul's request, Paul abdicated his request to be healed to God's greater purposes, and lived in the assurance that it would be understandable one day as to why God chose not to act in his case.

Now, of course, this harkens toward the old problem of insensitively—telling parents whose kids were victims of horrendous violence, or killed in a terrible car wreck, that God has a purpose for it and it will be understandable one day.

In theory, that may be true. But what is closer to the truth is that we live in a fallen world where God does not stop or prevent every instance of evil or fatal accident from happening. Love dictates we express only our confidence that God's heart is broken by the pain that his creation suffers in this fallen world, and beyond that we grieve with the broken hearted as Jesus did with Martha and Mary.

Because sometimes there is no ultimate plan—except for the ultimate plan from Genesis 3 where humans now have total dominion over this world, as handed to them by God when they chose to rebel.

Do we like car wrecks and children being victims of violence? No. So maybe what we should choose, and can choose for now, is God's rule over our inner-world until the time of Revelation 21-22.

S: Let's explore more about miracles and God's power in the next chapter.

D: Excellent. But first, I'm heading to get more coffee.

Scene 28

Without My Left Leg, I Now Walk With a Limp

D: I'm back.

S: So when I'm not here with you at Boffo's Taco Grill drinking coffee, I live in a country with *no* above-ground group of local believers who are following Jesus.

I and my friends literally live in a 'book of Acts' type of situation.

If people are going to 'come to Jesus,' they have the monumental obstacle of going against centuries of ingrained religious and cultural training that tells them unequivocally that Christianity is bunk.

We guests of the country often get together and talk about what it would take for a community of believers in Christ to take root there.

Someone usually suggests that a huge act of God's power might be helpful.

D: Probably couldn't hurt.

S: True enough. In the book of Acts, the same as in Jesus' day, huge acts of God's power were often manifested in the form of physical healings.

This was a beautiful show of God's power, as well as an awesome show of his love and care for people.

So in light of this, I've often thought, *Well, maybe I should get to know some people who have a sick relative and go pray for that person in the 'name of Jesus' and see if they will be healed—what better show of power could there be?*

D: Sounds like a good plan to me.

S: Wellllll.....no.

Because of the flip side.

What if I invoke the name of Jesus for the person to be healed, and the person is *not* healed?

What then?

Then I've brought harm and damage to Jesus' reputation that could take years for the people of that particular village to get over.

So my conclusion: It would be a stupid risk. Unprofitable. Unbeneficial.

Even more so, it shouldn't really be *my* decision whether or not to take a risk in that way.

D: What do you mean?

S: When miracles and physical healings were done through the efforts of everyday humans in the New Testament (the disciples and others), the people enacting the healing were told either by Jesus, or by God's Holy Spirit, ahead of time exactly what was going to happen.

In other words, they didn't act, but waited until they knew for sure God's plan as told to them by God himself.

I used to puzzle over the story in Acts 3:1-10 where Peter passed an infirmed guy on the way to the temple.

When the man asked for loose change, Peter looked at him and said: "I have no money to give you, but I do have this..." and WHAM! The guy was healed.

What a strange thing to say—"I don't have money to give you, but I do have THIS..."

And why did Peter only heal *that* guy on the way to the temple, and not some other random dudes hanging around?

I'm thinking now it's because somehow God's spirit told Peter *ahead* of time.

And this brings us back to why it is so important to make sure ahead of time that we know for sure what God wants.

Because if we don't, we run the risk of ruining, or severely damaging, God's reputation on earth, as well as embarrassing ourselves and making fools out of ourselves.

When God acts in human history, it's *not* willy-nilly.

Never has been, never will.

God has never been hap-hazard, and he never will be.

He's never been chaotic, or without direct meaning or cause, and he never will be.

When Jesus was fishing with the disciples, he never said, "Ok, throw out the net and let's see *if* we get something. If we get something, then 'Praise God!' but if not, well, then it's ok, we'll try again another time."

No.

Jesus never did that.

Every action from God is deliberate and has a purpose.

There is no 'hit or miss.'

So we see in Acts that when a healing occurs, the Sprit somehow notified the enactors ahead of time.

That is a good plan from God, isn't it?

And it has the added benefit of now that they know what the plan is, they know they will have the power and authority of the Spirit to do it, to go out and execute God's plan in God's power while they themselves are at 'rest' in their inner spirits.

Now there is never *any* embarrassment, 'practicing,' or failure on the part of God's people that results in a damaged reputation for God or ourselves.

As it should be.

In James 5:13-15, James was not guessing or hoping, but he knew ahead of time exactly what God was going to do. Therefore, he told them in full confidence what was going to happen.

"Bring the man forward and God *will* heal him."

Isn't it mind-blowing how good God is? That he didn't just say to those suffering persecuted people, "Hey, buck up! Be tougher! Live the truth and quit yer whining!"

No, he didn't say that. And he doesn't say that to us, either.

So here's another angle:

What about when 'healers' or 'people speaking for God' are sometimes *right*?

D: I've certainly heard of that happening.

S: But the problem is the 'sometimes.'

God is never sometimes right and sometimes wrong.

As we saw in the example of Jesus and fishing—there's no *if*.

If anything really comes from God, it is always always always always right and absolutely clear.

Unmistakable, and unmistaken.

Always.

There is no practicing, and certainly no getting things wrong, be it words spoken or attempted healings gone bad.

God never hits a bad golf shot. He hits the ball perfectly into the hole with one shot *every time*.

That's how we *know* we've seen God.

Scene 29

Bless Me Father, For I Have Misinterpreted Confession

D: I like what you said about God and golf. I have to confess, I love golf.

S: Speaking of confession, that takes us back to our discussion in James chapter 5.

In interpreting the conclusion to the book of James, it's very important to stay in the context of the entire book. James has a flow, a unity that's in agreement with the whole of the New Testament. Also, the book of James is logical and congruent within itself.

Contrary to James addressing the need for individual confession of sin, the amount of disunity and disagreement in the church was so explosive that he urges them—after they see the miraculous healing—to come together and confess their sin of unbelief.[1]

> Is anyone among you in trouble? Let them pray. Is anyone happy? Let them sing songs of praise. Is anyone among you sick? Let them call the elders of the church to pray over them and anoint them with oil in the name of the Lord. And the prayer offered in faith will make the sick person well; the Lord will raise them up. If they have sinned, they will be forgiven. Therefore confess your sins to each other and pray for each other so that you may be healed. The prayer of a righteous person is powerful and effective. (James 5:13-16)

Now, if we also encountered the exact same situation as the audience of James today, then yes, all these issues and concepts would universally apply.

But how many of us have ever walked down the street and seen the *Church of Jesus Christ of Following the Mosaic Law to Appease the Religious Elite and Mislead Them Into Thinking We Are In Their Ilk By Giving Them The Impression That We Get Right With God By Following Old Testament Rules and Rituals Independent of Any Help or Interference By God?*

Have we seen that church today?

No.

And why not?

Because of the book of James.

He wrote his letter to these churches for the very purpose of keeping them on the path of the 'Church of Jesus Christ' + nothing else.

Now, that being said, there are a couple of universal principles in this for our churches today. But it's not to confess your sins to one another and pray and be healed. The message is pretty much the same as every New Testament book:

1. Be unified in love as the church, as the 'body' of Christ on earth.

2. Do *not* make Jesus a religion. *Do not* make salvation and living the Christian life into Jesus + *anything else*. Stick with Jesus + *Nothing*.

And most importantly....wait for it...here it comes...Religion is *offensive* to God.

If anyone ever advocated for the eradication of religion, it was Jesus H. Christ.

As followers of Christ, we are FREE. FREE. FREE! FREE!

I will write it until the day I die. Freeeeeeeeeeeeeeee!

Step outside of your house right now and shout it like William Wallace.

FREEEEEEEEEDOM!

Really. Go ahead. Right now. It's ok. The neighbors already think you're crazy. So go ahead. Do it. Right where you live. No one will care, or think you're weird...much.

Good. You're outside now?

Then: *"FREEEEEEEEEDOM!"*

Paul says I am no man's judge, and no man judges me...I *don't even judge myself!* (1 Corinthians 4:3)

I'm free.

Totally free.

This theme of freedom is in every New Testament book. Please, go ahead. Read the entire New Testament. It's there. You will find it.

I guess this is where I'm supposed to say something like "If Peter and Paul, or even Jesus, came back today, they'd be appalled at the sad, sorry state of the church."

But I won't say it.

Why?

Because I don't think they'd see it that way.

I think they'd be ecstatically joyful that all the blood, sweat and tears they went through to start the early church has actually paid off. They wouldn't be bothered by all the noise like we are. They wouldn't be concerned with all the stuff that will burn up in the fire as so much straw and stubble. They don't see life that way. They would be ecstatic to see that in the midst of all that, people are still finding freedom.

That's right. *Still* finding freedom.

And if anyone wants to go back to religion, or live in their own power and efforts apart from God, then they are free to make that choice as well.

If you don't want to come to the party, don't come. But the more the merrier. It's going to be an f'n blowout, I tell you! It already is, and it's only going to get better and better and better.

Why would we need to confess our general sins to each other when we don't live in sin-slavery land, but are now card-carrying citizens of freedom land (Romans 6)?

In James, he was asking them to confess and be healed for a 'specific' situation. To be healed from their sin of unbelief about Christ + Nothing, and their sins of all-out commitment to self, resulting in catastrophic divisiveness and disunity in their community of believers.[2]

D: So if everything you're saying in this book is accurate, what about Acts 5, where God seemingly judged and cleaned house and killed people in judgment for their wrong-doing? What about that?

S: Well, first, it has been popularly insinuated that

God killed these people in judgment, but it doesn't say that in the text. Peter merely *foretold* their deaths somehow by the Spirit's leading. The text doesn't say God, or Peter, caused their deaths. The amazing thing to the people assembled wasn't that God killed two people in front of them. They were amazed, and had great respect for God, because Peter was able to foretell it. And not just once, in case that might've been a lucky guess, but *twice*.

Ok, let's look at some other things Acts chapter 5 is not:

This chapter has often been taught that the grace of God through Christ has made a way for us to be fully-honest about our failings and wrong-doing, so now we can, and should, air our dirty laundry before God and each other. (And God takes this very seriously!) We do this to prove we're not living a 'religious show,' and if we don't, we're being hypocrites.

So this passage is traditionally taught as an example of our freedom in Christ, but it actually results in the *opposite*.

Seriously, what good could come from people knowing I secretly fantasize about a tequila bender with Paris Hilton? Why would God want me to embarrass myself like that? (See Psalm 103:12, 1 Corinthians 13:5, Hebrews 8:12; 10:17)

D: Um, I think you just did.

S: Ok, but I did it to prove a point.[3]

So, again, it's commonly taught that the point of this passage was Ananias and Sapphira were not being honest about how sinful they were. They were trying to make people think they were better than they actually were (hypocrisy), and therefore, God wants us to air our laundry so everyone knows how 'bad' we are.

But that is far from the point of this passage.

Now, as a disclaimer, yes, we have the freedom to air whatever we want to before the church, or we can exercise our freedom *not* to. Whatever benefits ourselves and others. Whatever is most loving.

Now don't misunderstand. I'm all for confession and healing in whatever context helps someone the most. I can dig that.

But we need to understand that we don't *have* to.

The only confession of sin that is biblically mandated is the 1 John 1:8-10[4] confession where John says before we are made a 'new creation' by God, humans are 'sinners' with a sin nature and can't be perfect on their own apart from God.

But if we have a guilty conscience, and need God to heal us (and there is some process that the Spirit uses where all parties agree confession of sin is needed), then go for it.

Nothing wrong with that.

But we don't *have* to.

And more so, we do not have to have guilty consciences.

God already paid for it.

It's done.

It's *finished*.

The matter is put to rest.

Now, we may need to stop a wrong we are doing against someone, or make amends for a wrong we've done against someone in the past. In addition, it often happens that the very act of letting someone into our lives and struggles is the very act God will use to break us free from the grip of the wrong that's hurting us or others.

But again—as the Spirit leads. There is no carte blanche command to confess sins in the New Testament.

One reason I bring this up as a matter of importance is recently I've heard of the practice of engaged couples going through and confessing to a counselor every instance of sexual immorality committed before marriage.

This is meant to be 'healing.'

But is it? Is it even necessary?

Again, if it helps someone, by all means do it.

But we also need to understand that this can *also* do more harm than good.

Why do I say this? Because I've seen it happen.

Jesus did not go to the cross to take away sin so that we can then dredge it all up again.

It is done. *Finished.*

If couples struggle with their past, I fully believe it is enough to lovingly tell them, "You know what, God forgives your past totally. It's done. Gone forever. Taken care of. Finished."

It can be dangerous to give people the impression that unconfessed sexual sin will necessarily be a hindrance in their new marriage.[5]

D: I imagine what you've said isn't too heretical. At least not any more so than the rest of this book.

S: Thanks for your vote of confidence.

D: I'm kidding.

S: Well, now that we've seen what Jesus' true mission was, and how Paul and James unpacked it for us as believers today, it's time to wrap up our discussion for now.

---

[1] This becomes vitally important when we are interpreting verses such as Philippians 1:6 where Paul says, "I am confident of this very thing, that he who began a good work in you will complete it until the day of Christ Jesus." This has been traditionally viewed as a promise pertaining to an individual believer's 'walk' with God, which produced a theology where God has us in a process of 'breaking down the outer man' as we become more like Christ, and over time we become more and more 'sanctified.' But actually, the letter to the Philippians was addressed to a community of believers, not an individual. So it's probably more accurate to look at this as a promise from God to the community of believers as a whole. That God will continue to complete a good work in them as a community of believers until the day of Christ Jesus.

[2] I don't particularly agree with the The Message translation's paragraph break in James 5:16. The 'therefore' of verse 16 makes more sense in the NIV, making it more specific to what was going on in that particular church, or group of churches at that specific time.

[3] To Paris Hilton: Though the movie *The Hotty and the Notty* was panned by....pretty much the entire human race...still, I personally thought it was hysterically funny and showed your ability to poke fun at yourself while critiquing the awkward double standards of attraction, romance and

dating. Kudos to you, Paris, and if you get the chance, call me. D: I can't believe you went into an intellectual analysis of a Paris Hilton movie. S: Away from me, hater!

[4] Refer to Andrew Farley's book *God Without Religion* for an in depth explanation of why this passage is not mandating an ongoing process of confession of sin for believers.

[5] Now, I say 'necessary' because I do know that sometimes there are issues that come up that need to be worked through. But do this as the Spirit leads, not as a 'rule' or maxim to be advised carte blanche.

274 - /thē·*il*·logical/

Conclusion:

Where is all this going?

Power, Authority and Freedom

D: So you've successfully blown me out of all my boxes.

S: Hope it didn't hurt too bad.

D: No, quite the opposite. I'm really grateful we had this discussion. I must admit, it wasn't what I was expecting when you called.

S: We can get together again sometime if you like, when all this sifts out in your mind.

D: That'd be great, but for now, where's all this leading?

S: First of all, I think when deciding what is true of the world—be it religion or a philosophical system, or a secular mindset without God—we should ask ourselves this:

What has mankind always been searching for?

Is it not *power*?

And where do we find *power*? Who or what has *power*?

After all, who doesn't like power? Who doesn't want to be associated with or tap into whoever or whatever has *power*? The power to get things done, the power to move mountains, the power to heal and restore, the power to make my life make sense, the power to love others.

And secondly, who or what deserves to have *authority*? And where do we find this authority? What do we point to as having authority? And what authority can we comfortably put ourselves under?

Should the church have ultimate authority? A denomination? The Bible? Televangelists? Philosophy? Leaders? Men? Women? The Pope? Who has, or deserves to have, *authority*?

Jesus gave a succinct answer to all of this. He said ultimate power and authority doesn't come from, and shouldn't be ascribed to, anything other than himself.[1]

The Bible declares Jesus himself owns the rights to all ultimate power and authority. In Matthew 28:18 he said, "All authority in heaven and on earth has been given to me." Not to a person, not to a book, not to an organization, and not to any people within an organization.

If we are looking for power, look to the Spirit of God (the Spirit of Jesus, the Father, God, the Comforter, the Counselor, the Holy Spirit).

If we are looking for authority, it lies in the same place. With the Spirit of Jesus, the Father, God, the Comforter, the Counselor, the Holy Spirit.

Now let's ask ourselves another question:

As believers, what is the ultimate goal God has for us in this life? Why did he create us to begin with?

Is it a process of perfecting ourselves? A 'sanctification' process that over time results in us becoming more like Christ?

Or maybe it's to worry and stress as we strive to discover the one purpose God has in mind for our lives when he created us?[2]

Is *that* it?

Or is it something much different?

According to Paul, it looks like this: You are free.

And if you add anything to it, you are no longer free.

Anything.

So be free.

I wonder if when Paul said, "it is for freedom that Christ set us free" he meant something far greater, wider and more vast than we've ever imagined.

I've disliked using the term 'Christian' throughout our discussion. I did it for the sake of communication. However, let's consider that Jesus (God) never asked or commanded us to call ourselves 'Christian.'

Very early on during the formation of this new way of freedom, the followers of Jesus were labeled "The Way," then later called "Christians." But they were labeled that way by humans, not God.

Jesus came to earth, died, and rose again from the dead so we could be free, Paul says. So all humans have this opportunity.

What's true of Jesus becomes true of us (Galatians 2:20).

Jesus came out of the tomb and announced, "I am so unshackled, I am so free, that nothing, not even death, has mastery over me!"

And if we want to be a part of that, it's true for us too. We can have the pleasure and privilege to announce to the world: "I am so unshackled, I am so free, that nothing, not even death, has mastery over me!"

D: Wow. That's powerful.

S: We are free from all labels, groupings and categorizations: We no longer have to call ourselves Christian, Muslim, Buddhist, atheist, homosexual, heterosexual, American, Aborigine, slave, or Greek (Galatians 3:28).

God is not interested in labels, groupings and categorizations. God is interested in human beings set free.

Humans are the ones who've created all those shackling labels in order that we might make our finite lives in our finite world with its finite resources manageable.

But God set us free from *all of that* when Jesus died on the cross and rose again.

God invites everyone to jump on the freedom train.

We are free.

We are truly and totally free when we become children of the living God (John 1:12, 8:36).

Free from everything.

But especially free to love, be loved, to enjoy life and to have life and have it most abundantly.

I submit that the world is moving to a place it has never been before.

After all, has the world ever seen a 'free' community of people on earth, save for the few years following the coming of the Holy Spirit as recorded in Acts chapter 2?

And if we haven't, why is that?

The answer might be simple: Because we humans have an inclination toward religion. We can't help it. We love it. It's our nature.

With religion, we can control God. We can make God manageable and understandable.[3]

And each time the worldwide community of people who represent God on earth close off the *living* God with religion, God makes sure to burst out of it.

He did it in Jesus' time, he did it in Martin Luther's time, and he's doing it again...today.

Consider this story:

There once was a king who gathered his wisest advisors for a discussion.

Also present at the meeting was the court jester; the fool.

The king stood up from his throne, took a stick of chalk, and drew a line on the floor.

The king announced, "I offer half of my kingdom to whoever among you can make this line shorter without actually altering it in any way."

The advisors stood around rubbing hands on chins, mumbling to each other. In the end, they decided, "It can't be done."

The fool walked over, took the chalk from the king, and drew a line right next to the first one, longer than the original.

He received half the kingdom.

That's a good illustration of how most Christians view other religions. How do we compare and contrast our 'religion' with other 'religions'? How can we 'show' others that what we speak of is the one, true way'?

Should we do this by deconstructing all other religions? By showing those religions to be 'shorter' than ours? Should we embrace all other religions? Declare their validity? Is that the solution?

I don't think it's any of that.

Because God always intended for us to live a *third* line. A totally *separate* line. Unlike the way *anyone else on earth* lives.

We are 'new creations' (2 Corinthians 5:17).

We live in freedom (Galatians 5:1).

Period.

And within that freedom is the invitation to allow the living, loving, infinite God to live his life on earth through us.[4]

So the question we need to ask ourselves is this: Are we living Jesus as a religion? Is Jesus merely one 'religious' choice from a myriad of others on earth? Or are we living *something else entirely*, something completely off the charts, as God always intended it to be?

Let's remember the message the New Testament writers labored so hard to make clear to the early community of believers: Do not make Jesus a religion. Live in your freedom.

We believe the world will soon see something unlike they've ever seen before in the history of humanity.[5]

People the world over who are free.

[1] Matthew 22:29; Mark 9:1; Luke 4:14,36; Luke 24:49

[2] Something he apparently didn't think to make us privy to? Not very loving, if you ask me.

[3] We maintain our pride and show off our accomplishments when we strive to 'perfect' ourselves and make ourselves more Christlike, instead of getting ourselves out of the way in humility to allow the already perfect God to live in and through us. The former is done through religion. The latter is done through living in the Spirit as opposed to the flesh.

[4] This is what it means to be 'filled with the Spirit'— Ephesians 5:18. And this is not a command, or a 'law,' or a demand. We don't have to do it. The moment we are sealed with the Holy Spirit God will never look down on us, turn his back on us, or in any way view us in a negative light if we choose, in our freedom, not to participate in what he's doing. Our eternal destinies are not at risk. He will continue to be absolutely loving toward us and always act in our best interest no matter what we do. Nor is Ephesians 5:18 merely a 'suggestion.' No, it's not that either. What it is is what makes sense. It's an invitation to participate in what God is doing. It's an invitation to excitement and adventure. An invitation to literally and actually 'see' God. Paul and God know this is the best way to experience life, and have life more abundantly. It's our choice to participate, or...not, without retribution or consequence, save for what we miss if we choose to follow, and live in, our finite selves over God. God and Paul urge us to choose the most exciting life we can possibly have. Live in and by the Spirit, and not in the flesh (Galatians 5:16-18).

[5] Again, save for a few short years 2,000 years ago as recorded in Acts 2. And we don't mean an outbreak of physical healings and miraculous foretelling's of the future. That may or may not happen as a by-product of the work of the Spirit, or it could look like something completely different. It's God's choice, not ours. What we're talking about is a community of totally free people—totally free from the shackles of religion as well as totally free from the shackles of living in the limitations of the physical world in

our finite selves. A community not based on the religious plans, work, efforts, strivings and strategies of religious humans, and not steeped in mysticism or other-worldliness reserved only for the most imaginative among us. But a community of people living in the stone-cold concrete reality of everyday life who actually and literally live in—and are led by—the spirit of the living God. What does this look like exactly? Whatever God wants it to look like. The point is: We follow God. The infinite, uncontrollable, good, loving, and full-of-surprises God. We are along for the ride. We are free.

Acknowledgements

There are so many people to thank it would be impossible to mention everyone in these pages. It would fill its own book.

However, Melanie Harvey went so far above and beyond the call of duty we can never thank her enough. She literally took this project on as her baby. Her suggestions and edits mightily improved this book, and any clunks and bumps still remaining are entirely the fault of the authors.

This book was put together over the course of a year on two different continents and in several US states. Many people who assisted in this project live in sensitive areas around the world and would love to kick us in sensitive areas if we revealed their names.

The important thing is we're all involved in each others' lives. The authors have been privileged to have been welcomed and included in the lives of people who are—and always will be—better human beings than we'll ever be.

We saw babies born (not literally), marriages happen, divorces happen, took other people's pets on long walks and were invited to countless dinner parties and held discussions at innumerable kitchen tables and restaurants around the world.

We ate incredible food cooked by awesome cooks and drank way, way, too much coffee. We 'couch surfed' people's homes to the point of overstaying our welcome (we're thinking of you, Jeremy and Nancy Black and Larry and Julie Duncan). And yet no one physically threw us out on the street.

And for that, we thank you.

We hope to have many more years laughing, crying and sharing our lives together.

Thanks for listening,

-S. James and D. Harold

APPENDIX 1

We see in the Bible that not everyone was required to live under Gods Mosaic law. In fact, *no one* was, except the line of the Jews through Abraham and Isaac, the DOI.

Everyone else in the surrounding nations and people groups were totally free.

And what was the result?

Did other countries living under total freedom love perfectly?

Did freedom from God's law result in perfect utopian societies?

Well, I wasn't around at that time, but I think there were still wars and killing and death and robbing and cheating. And not only that, these societies were *burning their children on fire pyres in sacrifice to their 'gods.'*

Wow! Really?

Yes.

Can you imagine if you saw your neighbor down the street doing this?

<u>Scene</u>: *You're watering your lawn and your neighbor walks by your house with his three-year-old boy in his arms and a bag of charcoal.*

You: "Hey Bill, want to come over and watch the game

this afternoon?"

Bill: "Not now, I gotta go fire up the grill so I can put Johnny on it. I'm sacrificing him today."

Holy crap! You'd think. Or I'd *hope* your reaction might be even stronger.

Now think for a moment: Would it be right to turn away and let him do it? Or if he did and you found out later, would it be ok to hardly punish him at all, as in the example of the killer from Norway sentenced to 21 years in prison?

Imagine if they grabbed your kids and threw them on the fire too.

How would you feel?

What would you do?

Nothing? Is that your response?

That would be horrifically irresponsible and unloving.

But there were actual societies like this in the Old Testament. This is not hypothetical. There were people who actually experienced the exact scenario I'm describing.

And it keeps going:

What if all your neighbors came in your house and grabbed your children so they could mass rape them on your lawn? What would you do? Gladly hand them over, and be A-OK with it?

Well, this is the exact situation Lot faced in Sodom and Gomorrah, and yet we think God was a monster for 'judging' them, for putting a stop to it.

Really? Wow, how could we have gotten things so turned around?

How did we get to the point where we 'blame' God for doing something we ourselves would do in a second?

Anyway, so people in other societies were not becoming better without God's laws, nor, as we see in the Bible, were the people with God's law.

No one in either situation was getting closer to God, or closer to free lives, under the Law or without the Law.

So God made a new way. A new way for us humans. But he planned it all along from the beginning of the world that he would take the penalty for all our wrongdoing himself, thereby freeing us from the penalty of the judgment we deserve.

And it's clear now that we deserve it, right?

Even if we're Hitler or Mother Theresa.

And let's say Mother Theresa managed to be perfect her whole life, but the day before her death she makes one of her sister nurses feel stupid by embarrassing her in public by chewing her out for not putting someone's bandage on correctly. Well, she broke one law, so she's deserving of God's wrath. She cannot be in the presence of God with that one wrong on her account.

Yes, this sounds extreme and stupid, I know, but God loves us that much.

God is that detailed in how much he loves the nurse working for Mother Theresa. So under the Mosaic Law, Mother Theresa would be culpable. She would no longer be reflective of the perfect nature of God.

So, *thank God*, as Paul says in Romans 8, Jesus took

care of all our sin problem issues and now we are free!

Free to choose to live in profitable ways for us and those around us, or free to live in unprofitable ways.

It's our choice.

Does that mean it's ok now to go around punching people in the face and no one should have a problem with that?

Absolutely not.

Behavior, profitable or unprofitable, still has consequences.

Just because the sin no longer exists, doesn't mean that the outcome of those behaviors isn't still bad or doesn't have detrimental consequences.

God still loves those being punched and will protect them. In the meantime, or I should say, before we decide to go around punching people, God is imploring us to see the benefit in loving them instead of harming them.

What would that look like, you might ask?

This means I have a choice. In my finite human wisdom (flesh) I can go ahead and sock this guy in the mouth (unprofitable). Or by resting in the Spirit with all my needs met, I can decide to let God's powerful love flow through me to love this guy (profitable).

Now we are on permanent vacation, spiritually speaking. No kidding. It's really that good.

We still go to our jobs, to school, and achieve our goals. But now it can be done in such a way where in our souls and spirits, we have unloaded the baggage of every kind of fear and worry about our future, and other fears such as not being 'enough' in our relationships—fears of every single kind.

And its total. We are free in our spirits of every single negative thing you can imagine. And that free life in our spirits translates to our outer selves more and more over time. But it's never ever ever from *our efforts*.

We are free.

We are on vacation.

The only work we do is to get ourselves out of the way as much as possible and allow God to do his work, his will, his plan, through us.

More and more, as we learn to trust God, we become less and less fearful or worried about whether we will 'have enough' within us (or outside us, in terms of resources) to do anything at all. Because we know—and more importantly we know how—to let God's power and life live through us.

This is not theory.

It's real.

And this was God's plan all along, because this is how Adam and Eve lived in the garden.

God supplied everything for them to have abundant lives. And that is the life he wants us to have now.

They still planted the crops. They still went to work and school. But they were free from the worry of whether or not the plants would grow and be enough for them to eat. They knew the plants would grow. Because they knew God, and they had seen his power to accomplish things in them and in their outer worlds.

They trusted God.

They had faith in him.

They knew him.

They had FULL trust that he would protect them. Always. And always meet their needs no matter what their response, because nothing about God taking care of them depended on them.

APPENDIX 2

So is the narrow *gate* analogy Jesus uses in Matthew exactly the same as the narrow *door* analogy he uses in Luke?

Let's find out.

Luke 13:22-30 states:

> Then Jesus went through the towns and villages, teaching as he made his way to Jerusalem. Someone asked him, "Lord, are only a few people going to be saved?" He said to them, "Make every effort to enter through the narrow door, because many, I tell you, will try to enter and will not be able to. Once the owner of the house gets up and closes the door, you will stand outside knocking and pleading, 'Sir, open the door for us.' "But he will answer, 'I don't know you or where you come from.' "Then you will say, 'We ate and drank with you, and you taught in our streets.' "But he will reply, 'I don't know you or where you come from. Away from me, all you evildoers!' "There will be weeping there, and gnashing of teeth, when you see Abraham, Isaac and Jacob and all the prophets in the kingdom of God, but you yourselves thrown out. People will come from east and west and north and south, and will take their places at the feast in the kingdom of God. Indeed there are those who are last who will be first, and first who will be last."

Instead of being on the side of a mountain saying things about narrow gates early in his ministry as he did in Matthew, Jesus is now on his way into Jerusalem near the end of his ministry when someone asks him 'Will only a few will be saved?'

Most likely they ask this question because the Pharisees and other teachers of the law were teaching that Israel was God's chosen people. To use a phrase from a 2003 Chris Rock movie, their mantra was literally, "God bless us, and no one else."

Another possibility is that this person heard Jesus earlier in his ministry in his rallying speech give the narrow gate analogy that 'few will find it.'

Either way, we see in Jesus' reply to this person in Luke that he does *not* use the 'narrow door' analogy from Matthew to confirm the answer this person is looking for, neither does he reiterate his earlier Matthew point about few being saved by living perfect lives under the Law. If he *were* reiterating his point from Matthew (complete with its facetiousness), he would've answered, "Yes, make every effort to enter through the narrow gate (be perfect), for few are going to 'make it.'"

We would have expected him to say that.

But he didn't.

However, he does choose to use this same analogy, only he puts a slightly different spin on it. And with this spin, he changes the game.

He gives no confirmation or disconfirmation to the questioned asked, but says instead, "Make every effort to enter through the narrow *door*." (Emphasis mine)

So most likely they've heard the 'narrow gate' analogy earlier in his ministry, and they know that one. But now he speaks of a narrow *door*?

What gives?

This time, in the Luke passage, Jesus equates *himself* with the narrow door (a slight departure from the narrow *gate* analogy in Matthew).

By doing so, he identifies himself as being the fulfillment of following the Law to perfection, and thus what happened to Christ happens to us. What is true of Christ becomes true of us (Galatians 2:20).

We entered the narrow gate (accomplishing perfection) with him by being *completely identified* with him as the 'narrow door.'

Pretty wild, huh?

Secondly, in Luke 13:28-30 Jesus made sure to dispel any misconceptions of being 'saved' by proxy. Each individual is responsible for themselves. Family tree, ethnic line, or even being around Jesus, will not 'get you there' in the end.

Third, Jesus is once again lovingly warning those who are hypocritically following the Law that they will not 'make it' to God by the Law, just as he pointed out by using the narrow gate analogy in Matthew.

Now, after reading this interpretation, take a few moments to read the below 'traditional' commentary (the way we've always heard this passage taught) and ask yourself which interpretation makes more sense? What we've just presented, or the traditional way:

> Someone asked him, "Lord, will only a few be saved?" So he said to them, "Exert every effort to enter through the narrow door, because many, I tell you, will try to enter and will not be able to. Once the head of the house gets up and shuts the door, then you will stand outside and start to knock on the door and beg him, '**Lord**, let us in!' But he will answer you, '**I don't know where you come from**.' Then you will begin to say, '**We ate and drank in your presence, and you taught in our streets**.' But he will reply, '**I don't know where you come from! Go away from me, all you evildoers!**'

28 There will be weeping and gnashing of teeth when you see Abraham, Isaac, Jacob, and all the prophets in the kingdom of God but you yourselves thrown out. Then people will come from east and west, and from north and south, and take their places at the banquet table in the kingdom of God. 30 But indeed, some are last who will be first, and some are first who will be last" (Luke 13:23-27, emphasis mine).

Commentary on this passage from random internet site: Jesus is warning us in this parable that there will be a number of people who look like Christians, who associate with Christians, and who even think they are Christians, who will be shocked to learn that they are not saved at the return of our Lord. What a sobering thought. This text is not seeking to create uncertainty and doubt in the heart of the Christian. It is not seeking to rob the Christian of his assurance. But it is seeking to warn those who have a false assurance, but not salvation. In the last days, just as in Jesus' time and today, there will be those who appear to be Christians, but are not:

This random interpretation found on the internet is indicative of the popular interpretation of this passage. But this passage is not about 'people who look like Christians,' because those are *not* the people Christ is referring to in this passage.

Again, Jesus' mission was *not* to inform people how to be Christians, or to teach people how to be a Christian. This passage refers only to the people of the DOI, not pew sitters or nominal Christians, and that is the *only* meaning we should take from it.

Getting back to the original point that Jesus is not teaching the same thing in Luke as he is in Matthew-- Yes, these two passages have similar wordings, but very different meanings. Jesus uses these subtle shifts in meaning very effectively and smartly for his audience--the DOI. Actually, it's genius. He wanted them to see that to get through the narrow *gate* (perfection that is required of God-Matthew 7:13-14) they should identify themselves with *himself* (Luke 13:22-30, Galatians 2:20).

Ultimately, Jesus does answer the question of 'will only a few be saved' by implying that actually, the opposite is true. Many will be saved, just not what you'd expect.

"People will come from the North, South, East and West to take their place at the table," Jesus says, but "some who are last will first and some who are first will be last."

He couches his answer with the warning to the DOI not to think they are 'automatically' first because they are 'the chosen people of God' and 'descendants of Abraham.' Jesus lovingly warns them that if they follow prideful and exclusionary thinking that they are 'first' (and refer to other races as 'dogs' and treat them as 'subhuman' or 'nonhuman'), they will find themselves 'last.'

So we see Jesus' 'the first will be last and last will be first' statement is not a blanket statement meant for all humanity. It is a very specific statement to the DOI about their attitude as God being exclusive and exclusionary for *them*. In other words, "God bless us, and no one else."

All that being said, '*Will* only a few be saved?'

Jesus said people will come from the north, south, east and west.

That sounds like a lot to me.

About the Authors

S. James and **D. Harold** grew up in a traditional church environment, and since their teens have enjoyed many years in non-denominational and small group bible study settings. This is their first book.

www.ingramcontent.com/pod-product-compliance
Lightning Source LLC
LaVergne TN
LVHW011415080426
835512LV00005B/64